White SCHOOLDAYS
Coming-of-Age In Apartheid South Africa

Ismé Bennie

2014 Ismé Bennie
All rights reserved.

ISBN: 1500750085
ISBN 13: 9781500750084
Library of Congress Control Number: 2014916897
CreateSpace Independent Publishing Platform
North Charleston, South Carolina

For My Sister and Her Children, with Love

Foreword

The first memoir piece I wrote was called *White Schooldays,* and it sat in a file for many years until it was published by Canada's Maple Tree Literary Supplement a few years ago. Like most of what appears in my book (and that piece appears in some form in this book as well) it was about growing up in a small South African town in the '40s, '50s, and early '60s. Readers were invited to comment, and though most comments were favourable, I received a diatribe from one, accusing me—in summary—of being a white racist. I know nothing about that reader, but it was someone who missed the political irony of the piece, someone who did not have the historical context or maturity to understand that what we were then was the product of our times.

I have been trying to capture on paper the life we led as privileged whites, painting a picture of daily life as I remember it, with the hope that through my words and with the hindsight I bring to these memories, the political reality of the times emerges.

And as I write, I long for what could have been, a country of promise for all.

Contents

Foreword v

Looking Back 1

A Cold Wind 5

J Is for Jack. February 1980 7

My Father's Side 11

Visit from a Stranger 15

Being Jewish 17

Jews and Apartheid 21

Leaving Leslie Street 23

Our Household Pets 27

Tsotsie's Wedding 31

Daniel at the Drive-In 35

'You Must Remember This...' 37

Moving On! 41

Stanko's 47

Doblis 49

My Dinner with Mordecai or Judy Sums It Up 53

George or Holidays by the Sea 57

The River 63

Early Schooldays 67

High School	71
Taste Buds	75
A Religious Education	93
A Jewish Girlhood	95
Playing Fields	97
Extracurricular	101
Higher Education	105
Generation Gap	107
Residence	111
Friendship	117
Party Politics	121
Dan's Bar Mitzvah	125
Home Cooking	127
Local Tastes	129
Outside Influences	133
Appearance	139
Old Friends	145
Between the Covers or My Life in Books	149
An African Bibliography	153
The New South Africa	157
Epilogue	159
Acknowledgments	161
About the Author	163
Notes	165

Lightning zigzags across the night sky
It illuminates the city in sudden flashes
Lightning is part of me
Thunder is part of me
The smell of red earth after the rain
Is part of me
The release after the storm
The creaking of the roof
As the house settles down for the night.

Lightning zigzags across the night sky
Of another city
A far-away city
It illuminates that city
And strikes at my heart
I stand at a window
Looking at the sudden flashes
Hoping they will light the way home.

LOOKING BACK

We never asked about the old days, the old days in the old country. My father, who emigrated from Lithuania, never talked about them, and we never thought to question him. South Africa is where the family came to escape from a previous life, and they were involved in the now, enjoying the climate, the freedom, the plentiful labour, and the opportunities offered by the adopted land.

My mother was South African-born. Unlike my father's family, the Lithuanians, her family was originally from Latvia. But like my father's family, they, too, came to South Africa in the late 1890s to escape the escalating anti-Semitism in Eastern Europe. I knew my grandmother was born in Latvia and had come to South Africa with some of her siblings. That was about as much as I knew about her side of the family. My mother had visited relatives in Eastern Europe as a young child, but that was her only personal experience of it, and I don't recall her ever talking about it.

I was South African-born, but when I came to Canada where the question 'Where are you from?' is so much a part of the culture, it was almost too late to find out about my South African family's origins. There were few living sources, and now, many more years later, there are almost none.

I began to look back. I thought about names from my past and old references, family visits, details of long-gone events, and recalled fragments of conversations. I pored over the old photographs, letters, and postcards in my possession. Most of these are about my mother's family, the Jacobsons, and the search into my roots started with them.

I have contacted the relatives who I know of or I have been able to trace. I have scoured the Internet for details about my ancestry, finding out about my great-grandfather, his brothers and sisters, his wives, his children and their children, where they lived, what they did, and where they worked, and even some of their phone numbers. My Latvian great-grandfather was Moritz Jacobson, a manufacturer in Libau, known now as Liepaja. He was married to Berta, and after she died in 1935, to Klara. He had five children, three sons and two daughters, my grandmother Paula being one of them.

As I delve into their lives, I find out more about the fate of the 7100 Jews who lived in Libau in 1941. Over a five-year period, other than a handful of about 300 survivors, almost all were either deported, ghettoized, sent to labour camps, or killed in the struggle for Eastern Europe, first by the Soviets, then by the Nazi Germans, and then again by the Soviets.

I imagine my Latvian relatives living through this horrendous period of European history. I think back to my life around the same time in South Africa. My childhood years, the '40s and '50s, were a time when white children like me were enjoying a special childhood, innocent, uncomplicated, and unaware. The sunny climate allowed freedom of movement and enjoyment of the outdoors almost all year round, unfettered and fearless. We lived privileged and entitled lives, made possible by a racially divided society, with its black underclass. In those years I certainly had little understanding of the great racial chasm that was apartheid.

After I found out more about my Latvian ancestry, I wanted to experience Latvia for myself. Walking around Riga or Liepaja or travelling on buses and trains, I tried to come up with a picture of a typical Latvian but found there really isn't one. And I couldn't see myself reflected in the passing populace.

I came away from Latvia feeling very much a Canadian but still with strong emotional ties to South Africa, land of my birth. I miss the afternoon thunderstorms and the smell of wet red earth. I cry for South Africa, for what could have been. I look back with sadness at our ignorance about not just the state of our own country in those years but the world outside.

A COLD WIND

A story that came all the way from Siberia emerged from my research into my family's origins. It has helped to give me a new perspective on my life in South Africa during the apartheid years.

It is the story of my great-uncle Meyer David and his wife, my great-aunt Necha, known as Nany. Nany was one of my great-grandfather's five children and the only one who stayed behind in Latvia when the others immigrated to South Africa. She married Meyer in Latvia.

From fairly modest beginnings, Meyer became a banker, living a very comfortable life and travelling to fashionable spas until World War II led to persecution by the Nazis and finally deportation to Siberia by the Russians in 1950. It is from Meyer's letters to my mother in South Africa that I read about their lives of hardship and deprivation in the Gulag. Nany died in Siberia and has been inscribed in the Holocaust Wall of Remembrance in the Libau Jewish Cemetery.

Meyer was finally able to leave the Gulag, and poverty-stricken, he searched across Eastern Europe for a place to live. In his letters from Minsk and Tallinn and Nemencine, he always remembered the Jewish holidays and sent greetings to us. He asked for a *tallis* (prayer shawl) to be sent. In 1958 he wrote that he would use it for '*Rosh hashonna* and *Jomkipur.*' In the same letter, he says, 'In September the 15th we have Rosh-Hashana, this time for me the very hardest day, you start thinking about the past time, beginning from the time we left our nice home, together with my unforgettable wife, and now I have lost her...in this *yomtov* time you make up a Recapitulation of everything that happened to you....'

Meyer died on January 22, 1960, and is buried in a Lithuanian cemetery.

Researching the historical background to these personal tragedies, reading the letters themselves, and going myself to the Holocaust Wall of Remembrance brought me face-to-face with the atrocities of the era!

I was an ill-informed and unaware teenager, going to tea or visiting cousins, when Meyer and Nany were sent to a lonely life in inhospitable surroundings. Meyer sums up this ignorance in a letter to my mother: 'You asked me why we decided at that time—it was the end of 1950—to go to Siberia; cannot you understand it?'

I visited South Africa recently. I went to the Constitutional Court in Johannesburg. It is on the site of an infamous prison. The inhumanity of prison treatment, particularly for blacks, is recreated in a moving audiovisual display. I was also young when the evils of apartheid were being committed. As I went round the exhibit, all I could do was make up my own 'recapitulation' and think, 'How could I have been so unknowing?'

J IS FOR JACK.
FEBRUARY 1980

My father is eighty-one. He is Jewish, diabetic, incontinent, quite senile, and aware. He is depressed according to the amount of oxygen that reaches his brain, quite lucid when it concerns money, and aggressive to my tentative mother.

'Now you're the boss!' he says from the confines of his bed.

This is how I find him on a trip back to South Africa, flying in to visit him in 1980 after he had been placed in chronic care. There he is, being looked after by black maids—black women still the caregivers of the whites, when they are young children and when they become helpless old men.

He is in a special home for Jews like him. He is in a room with five other men. There is blue-patterned linoleum on the floor. There are six high iron cots with bars around them. A radio fills in time and space. Some plaster on the walls is chipped. The place is clean but worn and minimal like the lives of the people inside. The ward is marked outside with a large *J*, almost if it had been waiting for Jacob, known as Jack, my father.

All the men except my father have photographs of their families beside their beds.

I go to visit him each morning after he has been put into his chair. I am here in South Africa to see him. I come home rarely, only for illnesses and death. I sit on a stool at his side. A black maid in pink overalls mops the floor, and I move my stool from one side of his chair to the other as she sluices around his feet.

Like all the other visitors, I bring soft bananas. My father's lower dentures are broken, and it is difficult now to get them replaced. I wipe his mouth after he eats. His tea shakes and splashes in his hand and dribbles from his mouth. A bib is put round his neck. I look down to hide my tears.

Young black girls look after these old men. The men sit crouched over blankets or pillows. They moan or cry out. Their sons and grandsons drop in briefly to reassure them: 'Max or Sonia or Joe will be sure to come and see you this afternoon.' Down the corridor, sounds of sobbing women fill the space.

My father tells me he will be there for the rest of his life. He tells Zelda, the black girl who looks after him, that he did not want me to come home to see him like this. He grabs the newspaper I bring him each day and turns always from the front page to the financial pages. Last Sunday, I saw his eyes rest on an article about 'sex girls.'

The old man nearest him has on a woollen cap. He is almost doubled over in his chair. 'A thousand kisses, darling. Darling, please will you help me?' he cries to me or to Zelda or to one of the other 'girls.'

All his life my father has never had family photographs around him. He doesn't see the chipped plaster or hear the radio. But an old self can flash out. 'Talk about the Immorality Act,' he tells my mother, referring to the law forbidding sex between whites and blacks, as his hands wave at the group of old men and black girls.

White Schooldays

I slowly raise my weeping eyes. I see the hands of an old man groping across the floor to squash an imaginary *gogga* or 'insect.' Some days he takes off his shoes to do it, until the maid shoves them out of his reach. I see the six bags of urine. I see thin iron bed legs. I see my father's bandaged, gangrened, amputated, mutilated feet resting on a stained pillow, the uncut toenails of his exposed big toes pointing at me. I see a man struggling to get up, but he will fall if he's not restrained. Another man is hunched abjectly in his chair. Zelda sits on its arm. Her black hand gently and steadily strokes his tired thin hair.

Ismé Bennie

J is For Jack

*Jack is my father
Jack is in a room marked J
Jack is in a room with five others
Waiting for the touch of a black hand
The caring black hand
The hand that touched him as a child
The hand that touches him now he is old
The hand
That brings comfort
To Jack
And the other white men
In the room marked J.*

MY FATHER'S SIDE

My father was one of eleven children, six boys and five girls, who came to South Africa from Lithuania to escape the pogroms of the late 1800s in Eastern Europe. Their choice was aided by the strong potential for success in an underdeveloped country and the need in South Africa for fresh sources of labour. Like Ellis Island in the United States, the South African ports welcomed thousands of Eastern Europeans, and various attempts to limit the influx of Jews failed.

The original family name was Bene, but somewhere in the immigration process, it got changed to the good Scottish name Bennie.

The family came to South Africa in stages, my father crossing Europe to London on his own as a thirteen-year-old, then going on by boat to South Africa to join his father and brothers, though I am not sure where he fitted into the sequence. His mother and sisters and the youngest boy, Arnold, were trapped by World War I. I have a photograph of the mother, my grandmother, with the sisters Chaja, Chasse, Geitel, Gita, Leah, and Sarah and the young Arke, or Arnold, ostensibly taken to send to the men back in South Africa.

They were sent to the Ukraine for the war's duration and were reunited after the war with the rest of the family in South Africa in 1921. A ship's manifest has them arriving at the Dunluce Castle as 'Alien Transmigrants.'

The family arrived in the area shortly after 1910, when the four previously separate British colonies of Cape, Natal, Orange River, and Transvaal were joined together to become the Union of South Africa. The Bennies ended up in the town of Vereeniging in the landlocked Transvaal Province, an area situated between the Vaal River in the south and the Limpopo River in the north. Vereeniging was about thirty-six miles from the gold-mining centre of Johannesburg. It grew into an important coal-mining and manufacturing area, but when the family settled there, they would have had no idea that the corner property they owned would end up being in the heart of a busy industrial centre, or that their lumber and hardware business, Bennie Bros, would become the Saturday-market-day focus for farmers from miles around and the place where the black pastor of a nearby black township or 'location' would come with the Sunday collection plates' *tickeys* (three penny bits) and sixpences to pay for a new church roof.

I have no idea how my father and his brothers ended up in their lumber—or as we called it, timber—business. They must have had some knowledge of it from the old country, where they had been storekeepers of some sort, or so we believe, but it seemed an unlikely business for my father to be in, who was not at all handy; he couldn't even make a cup of tea, let alone get the fixings for his predinner Scotch.

Other than Max who lived in the town of Frankfort, the brothers ran the store: Casey and Barney managed it until they died young, and then it was just my father and my Uncle Arnold. Morris, the badpenny gambler they were always bailing out, helped occasionally.

The store was on Merriman Avenue, on the edge of the town. Close by was the bookstore where I secretly bought a book about

White Schooldays

sex education, and across the road was a patisserie, though that was not a word we would have used, run by a widow lady. She later moved it near where we lived, to Marks Avenue. It became a stop on the route home from primary school and my art class for a chocolate mouse. My Uncle Arnold and his wife lived in the same building until they had children and moved to the growing suburbs.

The front of Bennie Bros contained the hardware: nuts and bolts and screws and such. In the backyard was the lumberyard, with its distinctive smell of freshly cut wood. I still recognize it. When our house on Marks Avenue was built after the war, it contained only the best imported wood. My father would talk about the pine he was bringing in from Canada, and in the office was a wall calendar from a Canadian insurance company, Sun Life perhaps.

Mrs Groenewald was the bookkeeper; at the end of every month, she and my father struggled to find the missing pennies to balance the books. Her husband was the contractor who built our house. He ran off with their foster daughter, who was about seventeen or eighteen at that time. Mrs Groenie, as we called her, eventually remarried, and my mother and I would visit her in her new life.

My father would only employ women with good handwriting. Miss DeBruin was Mrs Groenie's successor. She was stocky and masculine looking, with short, cropped, wiry hair, and she wore suits and ties. We knew nothing of her personal life, and I had little or no knowledge of lesbianism in those days, so she merely seemed eccentric.

Stores were closed at lunchtime, and my father walked home and back for lunch until we got a car. One of the shop's drivers, first Jonas and later Daniel, would double up as a personal driver, taking my father to and from work. Daniel was eventually caught stealing from the shop, using the materials to build housing in a nearby black township, Sharpville, later to become known worldwide for the Sharpville Massacre of March 1960, when police opened fire on a crowd of black protestors who were demonstrating against the country's oppressive Pass laws.

Most of the time, my father was a genial man, but he had a short fuse, and in an altercation at the shop with a traffic policeman, his jaw was broken. He ended up at the university's Dental Hospital in the city. They discovered he was diabetic, and the large man diminished—with diet and medication—into a smaller version of himself.

He was usually jolly with friends and family and customers but could be difficult and short with my mother and nervy around his children. He would ask, 'Who are you going with? Why are you late?' I think he was manic-depressive and certainly as the years passed, just depressive. His depression may have been as a result of the money he lost when his platinum shares plummeted. He still invested in the stock market, played bridge for high stakes, bet on the horses, and, as stores were closed on Saturday afternoons, went off to the horse races regularly.

Many years later, when he was in chronic care, suffering from dementia, he told me about the horse he had owned. I have no idea if this was true or if this was a figment of his disturbed mind!

VISIT FROM A STRANGER

I was about nine, hanging around our front garden on Marks Avenue, when a long, two-toned, brown-and-beige American car stopped outside our house, and a strange woman got out from the driver's side. She was wearing a brown-and-gold tweed suit, and her reddish hair was tied up in a scarf of the same colours. She introduced herself as a cousin Toby, Abraham's daughter.

My father thought for a moment and then placed her. 'Abraham from Heilbron. Abraham Bennie, the cousin who went to the United States?'

Toby told us that her father had taken her and her brother to the United States in 1922 after her mother died. Her father was no longer alive, but there was other family in New York, the ones they had gone to live with. A whole chapter about my father's family was unfolding.

Our new cousin told us that she and her husband were settling in South Africa, in Illovo, a suburb of Johannesburg. He was Hungarian, and he was actually a count. Toby was a countess! We took this in for discussion later. A lot of dubious European counts had come to settle in South Africa in the postwar years.

This wasn't the first time a relative had come looking for my father. A stranger in a black suit approached my mother and me in Nairobi Airport, while we were waiting for a plane to go home. 'Do you by any chance know Jacob Bennie of Vereeniging?' he asked. He was coming to solicit funds for a religious school in Israel.

Obviously Toby wasn't looking for a handout. She was well dressed, had a big car, lived in a smart part of the city, and was a countess to boot. She just wanted to say hi!

My mother got pen and paper and took down Toby's details. I never saw Toby again. She wasn't invited to Bennie family events, not because she was married to a Hungarian or to a count but because she was married to a non-Jew. My mother was more open-minded. She kept connections. She phoned Toby every now and then, just to keep in touch. Fifteen years later, when I went to live in the United States, Toby gave my mother the name and address of some New York relatives.

I took the Long Island Railway from Manhattan to Far Rockaway and went to see them several times. The visits over an early dinner in their small apartment were not easy. They were a sad older couple, and we had little to talk about; I lost touch once I went to live in Canada. My mother would have at least been able to tell Toby that I had made contact.

I sometimes wonder what happened to Toby, and I am reminded about family attitudes and prejudices that prevailed in those days.

BEING JEWISH

We were Jewish. There was never any discussion about it; we just were. As a young child, I knew that it had its obligations: I remember asking, to my parent's amusement, why Jews were always being asked to donate money.

South Africa was far from anywhere, and the Jewish population was quite insular. I grew up in a small South African town, and I was the product of small-town life. For a long time, I believed that anyone with a name ending in 'sky' or 'ski' or 'vits' or 'witz' had to be Jewish!

In the years I was growing up, we were a close-knit community; the confines of a small town kept us near each other. Almost all the families on our block in the town of Vereeniging were Jewish: my family, the Hersches, Schmamans, Sacks, Slomowitzes, and Joffees, and there were many more Jewish families nearby. As the town grew and spread into suburbs, some moved on, but I am writing about the '40s and '50s.

We were not a particularly religious family, much beyond my father going to synagogue on the high holidays and occasionally getting roped in to make up a *minion,* the group of ten men needed for the Friday evening service. We never ate pork or shellfish or bread at Passover, but I think we were a little lax about mixing meat and milk dishes. We always had a nice Friday-night dinner with the candles lit and always had special meals on religious holidays.

There was not the population to support a Jewish school, so we went to the local public schools, and the kids—Jews and non-Jews—mixed with each other, though the adults tended to mix socially just with other Jews.

Keeping up with the family was important to us, perhaps being an immigrant family far away from our roots. We would visit my mother's various aunts and uncles and cousins in Johannesburg. We would have tea and cookies served by a black man in a white jacket at one cousin's, we would go to see her aunt Lily at her fancy apartment in a fashionable suburb, and we would drop in on a cousin Lily, who married well after many years of selling hosiery at a Johannesburg department store. We went off to see my mother's Pretoria cousins and went once or twice to Durban on the coast, where her uncle owned a hotel.

I would meet up with my father after his Sunday-afternoon bridge game in the city, and we would visit his oldest sister in an old, established Johannesburg area. Once or twice a year, we would visit one of his brothers and later his brother's widow Sarah, in Frankfort, a small town a few hours' drive away. After Friday-night dinner, I would go with my father to see his sister Annie who lived in our hometown just a few blocks away from us. We would walk over to see her and her husband Louis. The adults would sit and chat in the front living room, and I would visit with my cousins Joyce and Isador in the back.

There were Sunday afternoon tea parties with my father's siblings and their families; these usually ended up near sundown with a glass of Scotch for the men.

As we went about keeping in touch, there were some missing connections. My father's brothers, other than Casey and Morris, had all married. Barney married the postmistress of a nearby small town, but we never met her. She was non-Jewish, and the family would not have anything to do with her. They had a daughter, so I have a cousin close to my age whom I have never met and whom my cousins and I have not been able to trace, though we did find mention of a Bennie woman at a Buckingham Palace garden party for Commonwealth visitors. And the family would have nothing to do with the cousin from the United States and her non-Jewish husband who had come to live in South Africa, in nearby Johannesburg.

My parent's generation had escaped anti-Semitism, pogroms, and the like, but it was still in their consciousness. They were part of a small community of Jews in a new and different land. They had brought with them strong cultural and religious beliefs. Maintaining this Jewish identity meant more than maintaining relationships perceived as being detrimental to it.

And in a small town like Vereeniging, in a community where everyone's business was known, and speculation and gossip was rife, family indiscretions like marrying out of the faith were best kept quiet. Everyone just went on being 100 percent Jewish.

JEWS AND APARTHEID

Apartheid was flourishing in my growing-up years. Jews were widely thought of as being opponents of this system of racial injustice, their liberal values being deeply rooted in a history of persecution in Eastern Europe. But there was also unspoken support for the government, not wanting the status quo to be disrupted or the economic and social superiority over the black populace to be undermined. And some felt that the government's focus on the blacks kept its attention away from the Jews, who might otherwise be targets.

Many South Africans, Jews, and non-Jews, who could not accept living in a racially split society, with its black underclass, left the country. Some were forced to leave, to escape arrest because of their political sympathies or activities against the system; some had no choice about remaining, being imprisoned or under house arrest as victims of the government's relentless persecution. Many of the names of whites in the forefront of the struggle for freedom were Jewish. These names come immediately to mind: Ruth First,

Nadine Gordimer, Joe Slovo, Harold Wolpe, Helen Suzman, Albie Sachs, Dennis Goldberg, and Ron Kasrils.

Despite the passing of the years, the increasing international attention on South Africa's abusive racial policies and the struggles of those trying to change the system by treating black help with respect and sensitivity, even superficially, took a while to become common, and even then it was tenuous.

Many of my South African countrymen came to Canada. Not all were politically motivated to leave; economic concerns played a large role, too. One woman, a recent immigrant in those days, said she was pleased to be without servants: 'They eat you out of house and home. They put butter on both sides of the bread.' These sentiments may not have been specifically Jewish, but I was shocked to hear them spoken unabashedly by a Jewish mouth.

My father's brothers and sisters were Lithuanian immigrants. When they spoke amongst themselves, they spoke Yiddish. I know some Yiddish words like *chutzpah*, but most others that I knew have faded from memory. But a word I do know, I heard it often amongst Jews and still do, was *schwartze*, meaning 'black person,' usually said in a derogatory way. I cringe when I hear it come out of a Jewish mouth.

And now when on a trip back to South Africa, I visit an old friend or family member, someone with whom I grew up and with whom I have an almost identical background, and I hear the black maid being shouted at, my level of discomfort is great, and I find it difficult to accept that, in spite of shared childhood experiences, we still have such divergent attitudes towards right and wrong.

LEAVING LESLIE STREET

After my father retired, my parents left Vereeniging and settled in a residential hotel in the nearby city, Johannesburg, just thirty-five miles away. My father played bridge at his club every day until he became too ill and needed chronic care. My mother did the crossword every day and counted the hours between meals: breakfast, morning tea, lunch, afternoon tea, dinner, and bed.

Once my parents were no longer living in Vereeniging, I had little reason to visit the town. All that has remained for me of Vereeniging are my recollections of an uncomplicated childhood and youth spent with friends and family in its environs.

Vereeniging is situated on the Vaal, or 'dirty river,' and the town's emblem is a bridge of hands over the river. In my day there were two footbridges, one for whites and one for blacks, which crossed the railway tracks. They were on the route we kids took to get to the river, the town's main attraction for recreation and entertainment and our destination for all sorts of outings, as we took advantage of the long, warm summer days.

We got around by bicycle, riding around the compact, neat town, streets one way, avenues the other, and a ring of industries and a coal mine or two containing it all. After World War II, Vereeniging suddenly sprouted suburbs, unending areas of bungalows on half-acre lots, each with a child's swing in the garden and a water sprinkler endlessly moving backwards and forwards on a struggling lawn.

The house we first lived in was on Leslie Street. I don't know the number any more, and there is no one left to ask. The house itself was a one-floor bungalow, like most of the houses in small South African towns. My grandmother fed me on its screened-in back porch. I would sit on my father's lap in the front living room or lounge, as we called it, with its leaded windows, and spell big words—'accommodation' was one. I had my photograph taken there, sitting on the piano, a big bow in my hair. My friend Carol and I played there, planning our weddings; mine was to be a picnic, and we also played doctor. When I broke out in spots, probably German measles, I would not let the real doctor near me to confirm the diagnosis. At that time I was sleeping on a small bed in my parents' room, because my grandmother had the only other bedroom in our house. She had left the sheep farm in Colesberg in the Cape after her husband died and had come to live with us. That room became mine when she died, but I have no recollection of myself in it.

The servant's quarters were at the far end of the backyard near the outhouse. A sewage truck would come along the lane that ran behind to empty it, though we eventually got an indoor toilet.

Sarah and James were our servants then, living in the small back room. They were Cape Coloureds; mulatto is the closest description, with light-coffee-coloured skin. When my grandmother came to live with us, she brought them with her.

Sarah was a large woman, always with a *doek* (scarf) or a cap on her head. She was the cook and housemaid and my nursemaid, or nanny. She took care of me most of the time. The day my sister was born, she took me to visit my mother in hospital. I see her now, in

White Schooldays

the garden at Leslie Street, with a bowl between her knees, whipping cream into butter by hand. It was war time, World War II, that is. We ate brown bread instead of white and had tapioca instead of rice.

James was her husband, our houseboy and gardener. James's mother worked across the road, a thin toothless woman, also always wearing a *doek*. Living with her was Cookie, a little girl, thin with wiry hair, who was either James's daughter or sister. I don't know which. The adults had a liking for a thick, pungent brew known as kaffir beer and would party noisily in the backyard on Saturday nights, the parties often ending up in noisy fights.

Sarah and James came with us when we left Leslie Street and moved into our big, new, two-story house on Marks Avenue. I was about nine. I took my doll with me, a Shirley Temple doll named Mavis after the girl who lived next door on Leslie Street.

We got new furniture for the new house, and my parents got a new radio, not the black Bakelite box that sat on a side table when we listened to the news during the war. This was a real piece of furniture, a low wooden cabinet like a sideboard. It had a turntable behind one door and the radio behind the other. The radio had a shortwave band, and I would fiddle until I managed to find the Voice of America; I also had my own bedside radio now.

Our cats, the black mother and the grey kitten, my Smokey, also came with us to the new house on Marks Avenue. We put butter on their paws, supposedly to keep them from returning to the old house. And like the cats, I had no reason to go back to Leslie Street. I only do that in memory.

OUR HOUSEHOLD PETS

Pets did not play a large part in our lives in Vereeniging, the South African town in which I grew up, at least not in my childhood years of the '40s or '50s.

I do remember—though it could hardly be called a pet—the goat that my friend Carol's aunt had in her yard. I have absolutely no idea why she kept it. Carol and I played with the goat, but again I have no recollection of how. It was quite small.

My mother's friends, the Cogans, had a bird in a cage; it was either a budgie or a canary, the latter I think. It was rare to keep a bird. The Cogans left our town, and I don't remember anyone else having a bird, not in our neighbourhood at least.

We had silkworms as kids—again, not really pets. We kept them in a shoebox with holes in the lid for air. They started off as eggs, which we bought or saved from the previous generation, and after the eggs hatched, we fed the worms with lettuce leaves for yellow silk and mulberry leaves for red. Luckily we had a mulberry tree in our back garden. We cleaned the box regularly and eventually tried to spin the silk off the cocoons, and we saved the newly laid eggs for another generation of worms.

There was not even an occasional gerbil. Dogs and cats were the most common pets. The belief in our town, perpetuated by our black servants, was that the Chinese ate dogs and cats, so we were wary around the nearby Chinese-owned stores. We made little fuss over our cats and dogs. There were no fancy pet stores, no special pet foods, no pet baskets, no boxes, no groomers, no fancy breeds, no toys, or other special accoutrements. Cats were cats; they were nice to pet, but they were required to catch mice. Dogs were just dogs and were either playmates for children or were watchdogs, required to bark at black *skelms*, 'thieves,' and drive them away. Dogs regularly barked at blacks; in those days we thought it was instinctive, but I believe they just picked up on and reacted to the apprehension and dislike emanating from their white owners.

Some of my friend's families had dogs. Dorothy's dog had three legs, having lost one when he was hit by a car, but he managed very well, hobbling around. Our next-door neighbours had a fox terrier called Rex who hung around the block. One day he got stuck while having sex, much to the amusement of the watching kids. Myrna had an elegant collie called Prince. The two of them epitomized the idea of pets and owners looking alike, both slim, tall, and angular, with sharp facial features. Estelle had Binky Lou, the only dog that really fitted into the pet category. He was a Pekinese and small enough to live in the hotel suite with Estelle's family who managed the hotel. I don't think he was ever taken for a walk; I don't think any of the local dogs were. I have no memory of seeing dogs on leads being taken out for a constitutional. Mind you, most of us lived in houses surrounded by quite spacious yards. Vereeniging had very few apartment buildings in those days.

We didn't have a dog, though I remember an occasion when a local dog, not sure whose, stole the roast off the kitchen counter and was beaten, over my loud protests. My only other dog recollection comes from a few years later, while I was at university in the city. I went to a friend's family home for Sunday lunch. I wasn't wearing my glasses. Wanting to impress, I identified one of their paintings as being very Picasso-like.

'It is a Picasso,' said the mother, and I wrongly identified the large black Irish wolfhound in the garden as a cow.

Our family was always a cat family. My cousin Evelyn had a black cat that lay in wait to grab and bite ankles. In my own immediate family, my sister had a cat for many years, and she makes overtures at any and every cat she encounters and buys T-shirts or totes with cats on them. My nephew has Mr Minnie. My niece's husband is unfortunately allergic to them. I babysat some cats in my London years. The unfortunate Ramses, my cousin Yolanda's cat, died in my care one night, yowling for his owner. My friend Marian left her cat with me to look after without telling me it was ill, and I had to cope with yet another London feline crisis, though not fatal.

I haven't had a cat of my own as an adult. I broke ranks and had a dog in Toronto. Some neighbourhood kids were on the sidewalk trying to give a puppy away, and I succumbed and ended up with the bad Jenny for sixteen years, Jenny who stole hot dogs out of the hands of children, Jenny who is no longer with us. I would quite like a cat, but don't want to cope with the dreadful pain, as with Jenny, of losing it.

Smokey, the cat of my childhood, is the cat that has had the biggest place in my pet memories. I must have been about nine when we brought the black mother cat and one of her kittens from our Leslie Street house to our new house on Marks Avenue. Cat mythology said that putting butter on their feet would keep them from finding their way back. The kitten became my Smokey. Cats were put out at night to do whatever cats did nocturnally. Smokey sometimes came home with a torn ear. But like a cat in the verse from my childhood, the smile on his face 'was a smile of content.' He would wait for the maid to open the kitchen door when she started work in the morning, and then he would rush upstairs and meow outside my door until I let him in and onto the bed. He was a placid cat. He would lie curled up like a fat grey cushion, and my father would sit on him without realizing it, and neither moved.

We had other cats during the long Smokey era: Hitler, a he (or she) that had a black moustache; Sputnik, obviously a cat of those times; one named after a catty girl I knew; and one who followed my mother down the street like a dog. But these were outdoor yard cats. Smokey lived to a comfortable, ripe old age, long after I left Vereeniging for the city. He didn't come home one day and went off quietly to die when he felt his time had come. Like elephants, that's what cats are supposed to do.

TSOTSIE'S WEDDING

My mother thought of herself as a liberal, a relative term in apartheid South Africa. It did not mean she was at the forefront of the fight against the apartheid regime, standing in silent vigil along the roadside as a member of the Black Sash, which was an organization of white women demonstrating against the increasing enforcement of oppressive racial segregation. My mother treated our servants better than most and fed and housed them comfortably—all, again, relative.

We had several servants: Nanny, the cook/housemaid; Simon, the houseboy; Emily, the wash girl; and Daniel, the driver. Nanny had started off as just that—nanny to my sister Pauline, but as they shared a name, to avoid confusion, we called her Nanny. Almost every white family had a nursemaid for its children, someone who looked after them for most of the day and got them up, dressed, fed, walked, and delivered to the parents on call.

Nanny was promoted to housemaid when my sister and I were too old to need a nanny. Sarah and James, our original house servants, were then retired to Top Location, one of the nearby nonwhite townships. Sarah and James were happy drinkers. Nanny was Xhosa, religious, and went to church every Thursday afternoon with the rest of the maids, dressed in her churchgoing uniform of black skirt and crisp white blouse with a red sash across it. Thursday afternoon was the universal servants' time off.

Every day Nanny brought early morning coffee up to our rooms, a South African tradition. Cooking was part of her job description. She wasn't a great cook, but then we ate pretty routine meals, and it was my mother, like many South African housewives, who did the fancy stuff like baking chocolate cake, cheesecake, biscuits, and the traditional Jewish dishes at high-holiday times. Simon did the rough work, sweeping, polishing, and cleaning the windows. Everything got cleaned every day. And he looked after the garden. Emily came to wash on Mondays and to iron on Tuesdays, with her baby strapped to her back in a blanket. The laundry room was adjacent to the servants' quarters at the rear of our 'double-story' house (most houses in my hometown were bungalows in those years). Our servants' quarters were considered quite luxurious, with electricity and running hot and cold water.

Nanny and Simon lived in, but the driver Daniel lived in Sharpeville. Nanny had two daughters, Tsotsie (little rascal) and Girlie, who lived with her. It was illegal in those days for them to be there, but my parents left it alone, and I don't think they ever enquired who or where the father was. I don't remember Tsotsie's real name. The girls must have gone to school, but other than a memory of my sister and Girlie playing together as tots in our backyard, the next recollection I have is of Tsotsie being engaged. Nanny had been putting away linen and clothing for her trousseau, and this became a heightened activity as the wedding approached. The wedding was held on a summer's day in our backyard. My mother said it would be OK for the black guests to come inside to use our downstairs washroom!

White Schooldays

Colourfast

Monday is washing day
Emily arrives
Baby tied to her back
She sorts the clothes
White
Coloured
Black
She washes the clothes
White
Coloured
Black
She hangs them in the sun to dry
They do not touch
The colours must not run.

Tuesday is ironing day
Emily arrives
Baby tied to her back
She irons the clothes
White
Coloured
Black
Neatly folded
They have not touched
Their colours have not run.

DANIEL AT THE DRIVE-IN

We waited a long time after the war, World War II, for a car, one reason being that it could not be green, considered an unlucky colour by my mother. When we finally got our brown Vauxhall, my mother dented it on her first attempt to get it out of the garage and never drove again. A succession of drivers and brown cars began, a Pontiac being the next. Daniel drove us everywhere when he wasn't driving for my father's lumberyard (and later stealing from it). He took my father to bridge every Sunday afternoon in nearby Johannesburg, took my mother to visit relatives there, and even took my teenage friends and me to parties and jazz concerts in the city, patiently waiting to drive us home again.

We had two cinemas in our town, the Metro, where my friend Carol's mother was the cashier, and the Odeon. As young kids we went on Saturday mornings to 'bioscope.' Sometimes we played hooky from afternoon classes and went on Wednesday afternoons. As teenagers we went on Friday nights. We got a drive-in, and it became a Friday- or Saturday-night destination once we got drivers' licenses. Nothing was open on Sundays in those days. The Dutch

Reformed Church, the church of the predominantly Afrikaans population, was extremely conservative. Bars were closed on Sundays; even hotel lounges couldn't serve drinks, and no entertainment venues were open.

My mother, of course, didn't drive, but there was a film she badly wanted to see at the drive-in. She went through a lot of red tape to get permission for Daniel, her black driver, to take her to the whites-only drive-in.

After the show she asked Daniel how he had enjoyed the experience. Turned out he'd already seen the film in Sharpville!

'YOU MUST REMEMBER THIS...'

On Sundays, as Daniel drove us through the quiet streets of Johannesburg, taking my father to bridge or my mother to visit a relative, I would hear the plaintive sound of a saxophone. On a day off from work, African musicians got together in a deserted building to play jazz. The sound touched me, but I was too young then to know that I was hearing a cry for South Africa.

Music was around us everywhere. Our black servants would stand at the corner during an afternoon break and sing, picking up harmonies from each other. 'Kwela,' penny-whistle music, was a staple of street corners. The penny whistle was a cheap and simple instrument.

The first African music that was popularized came from the hit musical *King Kong*, called an African jazz opera. I had seen it performed in front of a multi-racial audience at the university's Great Hall, one of the few venues where blacks and whites could assemble together. The musical had an all-black cast, and it launched Miriam Makeba's career and captured the flavour and vitality—as well as the sadness and poignancy—of life in the black townships.

During the two years it played across the country, it was seen by about two hundred thousand South Africans, the majority of them white. It was a revelation to many South Africans that art did not recognize racial barriers!

But the music that has stayed with me all my life comes from the days after 1950, when South Africa finally got commercial broadcasting. Every Sunday night I would listen to the 'Bayer Hit Parade' on *Springbok Radio*, to Bing Crosby, Nat King Cole, Ella Fitzgerald, Frank Sinatra, Frankie Laine, Elvis, the pop singers of my teens, and whoever else had made it to the week's top ten.

I still sing along with these artists. I watched an old Glenn Miller movie on TV the other night and sang right along with 'Serenade in Blue.' I haven't heard it played in forty or fifty years, but I knew the words instinctively. And recently, in an art supply store, Ella and I sang together about a 'Nightingale in Berkeley Square.'

I was exposed to other sorts of music long before I got to know the pop songs of the '40s and '50s. In the weekly singing class at my primary school, I learnt the likes of 'My Bonny Lies over the Ocean.' But the ones I really remember best are in Afrikaans, the lullaby 'Slaap My Kindjie Slaap Sag,' 'Bobbejaan Klim die Berg,' 'Vat Jou Goed en Trek Fererra,' and 'My Sarie Marais is So Ver Van My Af.' Many of these songs originated during the Boer War and had political meanings which I wouldn't have understood in those early school days.

Of course we had to know the country's anthems: still 'God Save the Queen' in the '40s and '50s and the Afrikaans 'Die Stem Van Suid-Afrika.' I still know its words. It's only recently that 'nKosi Sikelel' iAfrika' has become the anthem of today's South Africa. Lord Bless South Africa! Through the apartheid years, years when I was away from South Africa, I would get tears in my eyes when I heard it sung. I still get emotional when I hear it: what could have been, and what might still be.

Jewish kids would learn 'Hatikvah,' the Israeli national anthem, the anthem of the Jewish people around the world. There were also songs incorporated in Jewish youth activities or in high-holiday religious services or sung at Jewish wedding receptions. I can recognize these, like 'Hava Nagila,' but don't know the words.

I was a typical teenager in the early '50s, listening to 'Hound Dog,' 'Pretend,' and 'Walking My Baby Back Home.' We would buy these records with their familiar labels, large 78s with A and B sides, a song on each. When I started going to evening parties, we would smooch to the slow numbers in the semidark.

'Cry,' 'All of Me,' and 'The Little White Cloud That Cried' were sung by Johnny Ray who was the Justin Bieber of my time. When he toured South Africa, my friend Shala's mother took us into the city, to the Colosseum Theatre in Johannesburg, to see him perform. Afterwards, as screaming hysterical teenagers, we rushed to the stage door to try to get his autograph or at least to get a glimpse of him.

I saw Danny Kaye, too, but he didn't create the same furor. A few years later, I went to hear Johnny Dankworth. A group of kids piled into our car, and our black driver Daniel drove us into the city to the band's outdoor concert. The boys in my group were into jazz. After school they would get together at someone's living room, playing the drums on the arms of their chairs as they listened to Gene Krupa, the Battle of the Bands, Stan Kenton, Jazz at the Philharmonic, and so on. This was the era of pink shirts and ducktail haircuts.

My only encounter with classical music in those days—hardly an encounter—was with Beethoven's *Fifth Symphony*. The local guys, usually the older ones, would whistle the opening four-note motif as they came by to summon us out. It was much later in life that my musical tastes expanded to classical music.

When I listen to the music of my youth, the music of my teenage years in particular —to those old torch songs 'Smile,' 'April in Paris,' 'September in the Rain,' 'As time Goes By,' 'September Song,' 'Autumn in New York,' 'Misty,' and 'Tenderly'—I am transported back to another time and place. They release a flood of memories about people or events in a time when I was young, and opportunity stretched out in front of me.

Buddy Greco's music sent me off from South Africa in 1962 to the UK, to another life.

MOVING ON!

I was never politically active as a student or in my early working years in South Africa. Like my parents, I was respectful of servants and black helpers generally, but any commitment to antiapartheid stopped there.

After working as a librarian for a few years, I saved up enough money for a one-way trip to London. I was not politically motivated, as were so many white South Africans at that time who could not live with the inequalities of a society divided along racial lines. My reasons for leaving were mixed; yes, I was aware of the government policies towards blacks and to those fighting apartheid, but I also knew there was another world out there, though not what it was and why I wanted to experience it.

So off I went on a one-way charter flight. My female copassengers put their hair in curlers and dressed up for arrival. Plane travel still seemed glamorous to us in those days, those early '60s. We grew up so far away from anywhere and were so limited in our experiences of the world.

Always being responsible and conscientious, I soon had a job and a place to stay, several different places for a while, until I settled into sharing a house with three South African 'girls.'

Through work, newly found relatives, and new friends, life in London slowly offered up new personal, cultural, and political experiences, though the last not in any radical sense. A variety of young people passed through our house for meals or parties; many were ex–South Africans with strong political beliefs. London was a hotbed of antiapartheid activity at that time, with so many South Africans—exiled or choosing exile—living there. I remember an Irish guy who was brought to our house. He ended up in South Africa, and we often wondered if he had been in the employ of the government's secret service. That question was always with us as we looked over our shoulders in those apartheid days. My roommate Judy stuffed envelopes for an antiapartheid organization run by a fellow ex-Capetonian, but that was about as close as I ever came to actual commitment. We were just liberal in our attitudes and our views. In any event, during those few years abroad, I experienced television for the first time, travelled in Europe, and left London to return to South Africa just as Beatlemania was taking over the world.

Like my reasons for leaving South Africa in the first place, my reasons for returning were not clear-cut, perhaps to compare and contrast the old life with what was becoming the new. I returned—not a different person—but certainly one with a broader view of the world.

It was hard being back after the freedom of movement London offered. Women did not go out at night on their own in South Africa. It wasn't a safety issue as much as one of perception. One went out on a date or did not go out. My friend Pam's mother would lock Pam in her room on a Saturday night so that visitors would not know she was home.

As for finding work, I became an editorial researcher for a newsmagazine. It saw its place as being centrist, bridging the Far Right *volk* and *vaderland* and the Far Left liberals/communists. It was an interesting place to work. It utilized black reporters and photographers on a freelance basis, it exposed me to world affairs, the small staff felt like family, and I had the opportunity to write the occasional article on subjects like the opening of a new resort or the significance of tattooing. I made good friends with members of the staff: Robert the film critic, with whom I went to the movies, sometimes two a night, and Harald and Ronnie, political journalists. I played bridge with Ronnie and his girlfriend regularly. Our fourth at bridge was Paul.

It was a period of great paranoia. There were many detentions and raids, people disappeared, there were dubious suicides, the government had spies everywhere, and one was unsure of whom to trust. My apartment was burgled one Sunday afternoon. The policeman who came to interview me about it seemed more interested in the books on my shelf than in the incident. Later, in a new apartment, I sensed that some of my things had been disturbed, namely an audio tape, though it was just a personal message from an old boyfriend. I was friendly with a journalist on one of the local newspapers, later finding out he was a self-confessed agent for the apartheid government, both in South Africa and in the UK, spying on dissidents and their supporters.

During my newsmagazine stint, I took a few weeks off to work as a researcher on a film being made about South Africa for US public television. The filming was quite overt, but all the time we felt we were being watched. The film's release (it later won a Peabody Award) and my involvement in it caused a flurry of anger in South Africa—as did any criticism—but by then I had left the country.

One day Paul did not come to work. He had been detained in police custody. None of us knew about his double life as a political activist. He spent several years in prison as a communist (communism was the synonym for any antigovernment activity), later leaving the country for exile in England where he continued to pursue his political beliefs. We were never back in touch. Robert and I had a little fantasy going that one day if we were both alone, we would move in together into a little rose-covered cottage. That never happened.

I left South Africa again in 1965, finally, for the United States this time, and it was many years before I went back for a visit. I always returned feeling some sort of anxiety, though my political involvement had been almost nonexistent. On one occasion, I was invited to Robert's home for dinner. By then he had given up journalism for painting. I was looking forward to the company of an old friend and his usual good cooking, but we ended up sitting in a row in front of the television set. South Africa had finally got television in 1976, and it became the focus of people's lives. Robert and I sat there watching old black-and-white US TV series. They predominated the schedule those days, as British and Australian imports were held back to protest apartheid.

I wrote about the obsession with television for the progovernment Afrikaans newspaper *Die Vaderland*, where I had reconnected with Harald, now enjoying a successful postnewsmagazine career. Some years before, I saw in *The New York Times* that he had won a 1969 Nieman Fellowship to Harvard, an opportunity to spend a year of learning and exploration and to return to his country to provide critical leadership to the press. I contacted him—I was living in New York by this time—and Harald, his wife, and baby spent a weekend with me. Ironically, a friend who had planned to go to an antiapartheid rally ended up babysitting for them.

Robert died in 2010, having become a very well-known painter both in South Africa and in the UK. I don't know what happened to Ronnie; he left the country, I should think.

It's hard to convey what that newsmagazine era was like. It is so different these days when I go back, back to the new South Africa. There is fear of crime and violence, political corruption, and huge unemployment but no longer that kind of political persecution. And wherever I go, I encounter black South Africans as my fellow shoppers and diners, taking care of much of the country's day-to-day business.

STANKO'S

I think back to my first day in London, the first day of that very first trip abroad. I was on a crowded London bus, and the black conductor shouted for us to move back. My hackles rose, an instinctive reaction from years of the white South African way of life. Who did he think he was?

Several years of living in London made me conscious of these South African reflexes, and I had a particularly heightened awareness of them when I visited South Africa.

On my trips back, one of my regular stops was to Stanko's, a small perfumery tucked away in a shopping arcade off Eloff Street in downtown Johannesburg. Downtown, in those apartheid years, was still the heart of the city, with department stores, theatres, hotels, good restaurants, and so on. When I lived in Johannesburg and went downtown, taking the whites-only bus, I would drop into Stanko's. Its owner, Mrs Stanko, stood behind the counter in the tiny space, dispensing Turkish coffees to her clients, mostly regulars.

I was one of the youngest regulars, enjoying the gossip about clothes and husbands as we sampled new products. The women who came there were 'European' in the sense that they were foreign, had accents, and were chic. They were very different from the run-of-the-mill mothers and aunts of my background. It was from one of these women that—several years later—I sublet an apartment while she was off to Bermuda visiting her son, who, like many of my generation, had started the exodus out of South Africa to more politically viable climes. This was in the late '50s.

In those days, one could order from Mrs Stanko by phone, and she would have Elias, the black 'boy,' deliver our purchases of creams, lotions, or perfumes, by bicycle to those of us who worked downtown or lived close by.

Stanko's was still in the same location when I visited it through the years. Now, though, the white consumers shopped at the new and safer suburban centres that had sprung up, as growing violence and crime took their toll on the once-vibrant city centre. My mother would still make the effort to go into town to drop into Stanko's and spend a few rand, and whenever I was in South Africa, I would always make a point of going to see Mrs Stanko, saddened by her diminished circumstances.

These visits were to a changing city, the changes more noticeable each successive visit. New highways carved it up, new suburbs extended it, windows were heavily barred, beggars accosted one at intersections, cars were being hijacked, and tourists were being mugged.

But what had not changed was that Elias, the 'boy,' now an old black man, was still helping Mrs Stanko, helping her eke out a living in a now-deteriorated part of town that could barely support her business!

DOBLIS

I had not had much experience with perfume until I started visiting the small cosmetics boutique at Stanko's. I knew the popular Evening In Paris, in its distinctive, dark-blue bottle, and Yardley's English Lavender, which I still associate with old ladies. These were drugstore purchases. Chanel N° 5 was one of the few expensive and recognizable French names. My mother had a bottle, going stale by being saved.

But my visits to Stanko's opened me up to new pleasures. Through the Stanko years, I wore Arpège, L'Air Du Temps, Je Reviens, Cabochard, Amazone, and Yves Saint Laurent's then controversially named Opium. I think I tried one or two Guerlains, but never Shalimar, as I could not get rid of its cloying smell from a sweater I loaned to a friend. Patchouli reminds me of it, though in those prehippy days, we hadn't heard of it.

Some of my friends also bought from Mrs Stanko. I have been in touch recently with Aviva, who left South Africa for Israel with her family and now lives in Chicago, and Tanja, who returned to South Africa after her travels abroad. I asked Aviva what she remembered:

'I went a few times with Tanja who was a regular customer—I think she knew Mrs Stanko personally, as they were both from Yugoslavia. I remember Mrs Stanko dabbing some divine-smelling perfume on my wrist, and I couldn't, for the life of me, remember afterwards what perfume it was. I also remember her telling me how to apply cream around the eyes.'

I also asked my cousin Evelyn in Cape Town what she recalled. 'She said my skin was no good for perfume. All my life I have tried to find a perfume, but after a few minutes, all I end up with is a chemical smell.'

Men did not use perfumes or colognes much in those days. The aftershave Old Spice was the prevalent male smell for a long time.

I was using Le De when I went off to live in London, but Bandit— in its distinctive yellow box—is the perfume I associate with my London years. I had bought it on a visit to Paris. Bandit eventually got replaced by other perfumes and disappeared from my life and from shelves. Several decades later I found it in a store near Barney's in New York City and bought it, but somehow it didn't smell the way I remembered.

While I was living in London, I house-sat for my cousin Yolanda. She often travelled, either for her work as a stage designer or to visit one of her gentleman friends. I introduced myself to her when I first arrived in the UK, and the relationship opened up new experiences for me in ballet, opera, and theatre—I saw the original *Oh! What a Lovely War* with her and heard about Nureyev's arrival in London. Her house was pure Miss Havisham, filled with dusty bric-a-brac: feathers, fabrics, rugs, and artwork, the detritus of costumes past and the stuff of costumes to be.

Yolanda lived a highly charged life, lots of crises and dramas, and sometimes when she felt low, I had to read to her at her bedside. When I stayed at her house, I would occasionally wear her leather jacket, and I would dab on some of her Doblis. I loved the subtle fragrance; it conjured up rich leather, aromatic tobacco, and exotic lands.

But like Bandit, Doblis also disappeared. Not that I had ever bought any for myself. But the memory of its distinctive fragrance has always stayed with me. When I close my eyes and imagine its heady aroma, it brings back memories of London. So does the odd scented candle or spray I sometimes use, perhaps from Penhaligon's or Floris from the UK. It recalls my friend Suzy's apartment on Sloane Square, where through the years I enjoyed so much hospitality. In the early '70s, it was a remnant of swinging London, with a changing cast of characters that included trendy hairdressers, actors, artists, impresarios, young lovers, psychotherapists, an improvident ex-husband, the odd aristocrat or two, and friends who frequented Annabel's.

In those heady days, I had no idea that my time in London and chance encounters there would eventually connect to my South African and Toronto life.

MY DINNER WITH MORDECAI OR JUDY SUMS IT UP

I have lunch twice a year around our birthdays with my friend Brenda. We grew up in South Africa, and she is the only friend from those days that I have here in Toronto. We lived on the same street in the town of Vereeniging. We went to the same primary school, the same high school, and also the same university. She is a year older and was a year ahead of me. But as kids we cycled together to the library in the afternoon, and she stopped on the way home for some of my mother's chocolate cake. We shared a love of reading, in our teenage years, of Mills and Boon romances. When we meet now, fifty or so years later, we don't have much that's current to talk about. She's married; I'm not. I go to the movies; she doesn't. She believes in the afterlife; I don't. So we reminisce about our childhood, and we exchange information about friends from the past. But we both still love reading. We talk about books. We arrive with our little notebooks filled with lists of what we've read and titles to recommend to each other. She goes to the library; I buy books. We both read much of what comes out of South Africa. She reads more nonfiction than I do.

At our last lunch, she told me how much she had enjoyed the recent biography of Mordecai Richler. So of course I had to throw in the story of my one encounter with our famous Canadian author.

As I started telling her about it, she stopped me and said, 'But that's in the book!' No, she hadn't heard me tell the story before; it was in the book!

Of course I had to read it for myself. I could not wait to start reading. The incident I was looking for happened in 1962 or 1963. But as I kept reading about Richler's life, I got well past the '60s without finding my story. Then, finally, on page 448 there it was. What was the author's source? Who had passed it on to him? I certainly had not.

I was able to get in touch with Charles Foran, the Richler biographer, through the kind offices of a colleague at the book's publisher, Knopf Doubleday Publishing Group. And Charles Foran generously offered to answer my query.

'Who told you about the London dinner party you describe?' I asked him.

The essence of it was that when Mordecai became belligerent in company, his wife Florence would find a way of rescuing him. In the book, Foran mentions a dinner party in London at which Florence called the babysitter to summon them home.

That actually happened in 1962 or 1963 at a house I was sharing. I gave Foran the details of what had transpired. I was sharing a house at 13A Gilston Road in South Kensington with two girls—I guess we were 'girls' then, in our early twenties. One was Judy, a large bespectacled girl, who, like me, was from South Africa.

While we were living together, she pursued the guitarist Julian Bream, who drank at our local pub. I remember Judy riding her bicycle to Julian Bream's house in Chiswick. He put her right back on it and turned her round for home! She would buy tickets to hear him perform at charity events at stately homes. Her father was a shoe manufacturer in Cape Town, and Judy would get a regular care package of shoes from him. Now I, on the other hand, had designer shoes courtesy of a friend who decorated windows for, I believe it was, Charles Jourdan in London. Judy wanted to borrow a pair to wear to one of Bream's concerts. I said no; I just couldn't bear to think of her plump feet in my elegant shoes!

Judy had read Mordecai Richler somewhere and had fallen in love with his writing. She managed to track him down and invited him to dinner! And he accepted! I don't know what the enticement was. Our pub round the corner, Finches, had its share of artsy types—Dominic Behan, Brendan's brother, the Canadian painter William Thomson, and the aforementioned Julian Bream who eventually ran off with Bill Thomson's wife, etc. I don't recall Judy's invitees, maybe also the writer Bernice Ruben. I was seeing a BBC radio drama director at that time, and he refused to join me on this 'blind' date. For Judy, this may have diminished the value of the promised guest list. Ultimately it didn't deliver to the guest of honour, who was, according to Charles Foran, 'curious to meet people of interest and import.'

Judy cooked like mad for the dinner—I still remember the heavy menu—French onion soup, boeuf bourguignon, and a rum pie. On the evening in question, the Richters arrived, Florence in the equivalent of a little black dress. They took one look at the group sitting stiffly in a circle of hard chairs round the room, and Florence, embarrassed by the whole thing, made for the phone, tucked out of the way in an alcove near where I was sitting. She called home, and I heard her ask the babysitter to call back in a few minutes and summon them back because of an emergency with a child. They left without eating. To this day, I regret not disconnecting the phone—having got themselves into this, they could have at least have had the good manners to stay until dessert!

Foran responded to my description of the evening:

That's a good story, thanks, one I hadn't heard before. Florence told me the tale I used in the book. At a guess, she used the 'phone call from babysitter' ruse more than once over the years or at least while the kids were still young. The menu certainly sounds right for the era—a rum pie! Best wishes, Charlie F

I have been in touch with Judy occasionally through the years. She married an Israeli film director and has lived in both Israel and the United States. They visited me in Toronto once.

I wondered about the guest list and sent Judy a 'memory lane' e-mail about the Mordecai Richler biography: 'Has to be your invitation to Gilston Road? I have been trying to recall who else was present that evening. Do you remember?'

And she replied:

I remember it to my chagrin! The late Ronald Segal (anti-apartheid exile) was there. So was Mel Boyaner, a well-known Montreal lithographer, also Jeanne Mance, who was a furrier before he turned artist and whose younger brother was a contemporary of Mordecai Richler, and Bernice Rubens. I can't imagine what I was thinking of, getting so many quite competitive people together with so little achievement to offer. Oh well!

I often think of you.

GEORGE OR HOLIDAYS BY THE SEA

Judy and I both happened to be in Cape Town one summer. I had Friday-night dinner at Judy's family's home. She was visiting them between her return from London and finally settling in Israel. I was in South Africa between my return from London and my departure—final—for the United States.

Cape Town to me is the most beautiful city in the world, and I remember this and all my visits to it.

The first visit would have been when I was about nine. My whole family went by steam train, a two-day journey, to Muizenberg, a few miles outside the city of Cape Town. Muizenberg was the vacation preserve of South African Jews, much like the Catskills for New Yorkers but without the entertainment factor! Our black maid came with us to look after my sister who was a toddler then, and she would have been accommodated in the hotel's servants' quarters. The hotels in Muizenberg were barely two-star, but people went year after year and stayed in the same hotel year after year. Not my mother. After this first family holiday in Muizenberg and our stay at the Marine Hotel, she would never go back!

After that holiday, my father went to Muizenberg on his own. He would bring back gifts for my sister and me—one year, sweaters, another time, the pin-on 'nurse's watch,' which I had requested. When I was about eleven, I started going to Muizenberg with my father, just the two of us. We would go on the Blue Train, a luxury express with everything—sheets, blankets, towels—decked out in blue. We shared a compartment upholstered in blue leather with its own blue washroom. We dined elegantly in the dining car, sitting on blue banquettes and eating off blue table linen. It always reminded me of an Afrikaans poem that I had learnt at school, about a small girl standing at dusk beside a lonely candle-lit tent looking out *'in stomme bewond'ring.'* She was looking with wonderment at a brightly lit train racing by, envying the sparkling wines and expensive food being enjoyed within!

The Blue Train was electrified, but as it approached the mountain range, it was hitched to a steam train to pull it over the passes, and then it made the descent into the low-lying Cape Town and its environs. In Cape Town we switched to the local train that would take us to Muizenberg and to our accommodation, my father and I now staying in the somewhat better Bayview Hotel.

When I first went to Muizenberg as a child, I walked for miles along the beach, looking for Snake Park, not realizing that it was the name of a crowded triangle of beach, edged by a row of bathing huts on one side and the concrete wall of a promenade on another, where all the young people hung out. The air in Muizenberg was invigorating and full of saline, and the sea had breakers to jump or surf. One could stay in for hours. But Snake Park had the attraction, once we reached the dating age, of putting girls and guys in close quarters, hoping to get a date or at least a relationship for the few weeks of vacation.

White Schooldays

In these Muizenberg years of my teens, I hung out with my friends from home or with friends made during previous vacations. In the evening after dinner at our hotels, we would meet to walk along the Promenade, the long, elevated concrete walkway that ran parallel to the beach. We paraded up and down, a few girls together or a few guys together.

New Year's Day usually fell during the weeks of summer vacation, and I did go one New Year's Eve with a group of friends to the midnight show of *Jailhouse Rock*.

As an adult, I went to Cape Town most years for my summer holidays, going to the beach, Clifton Beach, every day. Set at the bottom of a rocky cliff, it was divided naturally into four minibeaches or bays: from Fourth, which was the family beach, to First, which was for the older set. One clambered down steep steps set in the rocks to these enclaves, each year or so moving on and up to a more age-appropriate beach. My friends and I would skip the one known to be the Afrikaans intellectuals' hangout. Pleasantly tired, tanned, glowing with sun and salt, we would leave the beach to shower and change for an evening out at a party or a club.

Sometimes the party might be in one or another of the cottages perched along Clifton's steep inclines or in an apartment in one of the luxury blocks at the top. This was in the apartheid era, of course, and these buildings and the hotels, restaurants, beaches, and clubs were for whites only. There were a few night spots that fell under the radar, though. We felt quite adventurous patronizing them. Navigator's Den was one, a low-down, multiracial dive on the docks.

Going by air was now the way I usually travelled to the Cape, and even my father did these days. But occasionally I would cadge a ride from friends, and we would drive the one thousand miles, stopping briefly en route at the Colesberg Hotel for a drink or a bathroom visit. The hotel was like a stagecoach inn of the days of yore. The village of Colesberg itself was in the middle of the semidesert called the Karoo, and there were miles of nothing on either side of it. Once in Cape Town, I would have to start canvassing for a ride home.

Some years ago, in the new postapartheid South Africa, I had a strong yen to return to Cape Town, and so I rented a cottage on Clifton Beach for a few weeks. My sister and her family joined me, and we enjoyed beautiful weather, scenic drives, and idyllic days on the beach, descending from our cottage to the sea and sand below, sunbathing and taking the odd dip into the freezing-cold Atlantic Ocean to cool off. Even in this new era of South Africa, it felt as though nothing had changed. Our beach was still populated by whites, and the cars outside the luxury apartment blocks were high-end BMWs or Mercedes. There was plenty of black domestic help available. The cottages were white-owned, but—one change since I last visited—many had been rebuilt or renovated into luxury summer retreats with swimming pools.

In the evening we would barbecue or *braai* in an outdoor stone pit. I would give the leftovers to George, the black 'boy' who came with the rental. He maintained the property for the owners in addition to his day jobs. George had a room with its own entrance in the basement of the cottage. When I left, I gave him the contents of the refrigerator. I heard later from the owner that he said I had been the best 'missus.'

The following Christmas I sent George a *bonsella*, or 'gift,' of some money, care of the cottage owner. She later sold the cottage, but the annual gift has continued via George's subsequent employers through the years.

His current employer, almost twenty years later, told me George was seriously ill in hospital in the Eastern Cape, the area where he came from and to which he returned every Christmas. George, the 'boy,' was by now a man well into his sixties. He had held down manual jobs, several at a time. He was barely literate and unable to communicate directly with me except for one awkwardly printed thank you. But he had saved his *bonsellas* to put his daughter through university, and she was now an accountant, and he was educating a second daughter. This, his life in Cape Town, had been playing out through those years I was enjoying the sun and sea.

THE RIVER

South Africans who lived in the landlocked Transvaal or Free State Province or families from as far afield as the Belgian Congo and Northern Rhodesia, as they were then called, would make for the coast for their holidays. Those of us living in Vereeniging would go east in July, replacing the chilly Highveld with the semitropical Natal. In December we'd go south to the beautiful Cape, enjoying either the Atlantic or the Indian Oceans that frame the tip of Africa.

Vereeniging had its own bit of water, though. It was the Vaal River, which provided much of our entertainment and recreation in our growing-up years.

As kids for something to do on an afternoon, we would cycle to the Riviera Hotel, situated on its banks, carrying our bikes over the whites-only railway bridge or taking the long way round via an underpass.

The Riviera Hotel was a resort hotel on the riverbank. People, mostly from the nearby city, would come for a weekend. It had terraced lawns going down to the water, a swimming pool, and a dock. Often, on a Sunday afternoon, local families would come to the hotel for afternoon tea, served with scones with cream and strawberry jam.

A group of guys from the city kept speedboats at the dock, spending their weekends water-skiing on the river. There was also a motorboat at the dock, with rows of seats and open windows. For a small fee, one could go for a slow ride upriver and back. This was mostly for kids.

The hotel was also a place for weddings, one of the nicer places in our town. My Aunt Leah got married there one Sunday afternoon and so did Rosalie, one of the local girls my age. A dance was held at the hotel every Saturday night. As we grew older and had dates, some of whom drove in specially from the city to take us out, we would dress up for the evening, reserve a table, and dance to a small band.

After my friend Dorothy got her driver's license, she would fetch me, and we would spend the day at the hotel pool. This was during our summer vacations, when I was home from university and, in her case, teachers' training college. We would lather Brylcreem on our bodies, believing it would help our tans. We would order drinks, usually a local beverage called cola tonic, and for lunch, sandwiches from a hotel waiter. We would drive home tired and sunburnt.

Next to the Riviera Hotel was the Vereeniging Country Club, where local members played golf or bowls and went for Saturday-night dinners. My friend Estelle had a crush on the local golf pro, and I went with her to her golf classes. He was improving her swing!

In one direction from the hotel was the Vaal Dam, source of our water and another place for sailing or water sports. One year it overflowed, and the river flooded our suburbs. My uncle's house was under water to the top of the first floor, and his family had to live in an apartment until the water damage was repaired.

There was a ferry across the river, and it was another attraction for a family outing. There was an art gallery along the river nearby. It was a remote location for a gallery, and it was the only real cultural spot in our area. Our driver Daniel took my mother to visit it every now and again, and she bought a painting or two.

Vosloo Park was a large area on the river set up for picnicking amongst the trees and bushes. Black staff maintained fires for barbecuing or for heating the tea kettle. There was an island in the middle of the river, and the riverbanks made an amphitheatre. I saw a ballet performance on the island and also a national celebration, with a choir dressed in the colours of the flag. My cousin Isie would come from the city with a couple of friends to fish at Vosloo Park, and I would join them for a day of doing nothing much. On the last day of high school, my classmates planned an all-night stay at the park, but somehow that fizzled out, and we were home in good time.

What I remember most about Vosloo Park are the family picnics. These usually took place on Christmas or Boxing Day, or perhaps New Year's Day. This was in the southern hemisphere, of course. My father's sisters and their families would come from the city, laden with folding chairs, blankets, food containers, cake tins, and watermelons, etc., and join us, the local relatives. We would spend the day together, kids playing and parents relaxing. My father's sisters were very close and would huddle together for a day's gossip.

Years later, the girl cousins of an age bonded like our aunts. We told each other things that we never told our mothers: about our step-cousin who, when the girl cousins were younger, had us listen to pornographic records, gave sex education talks, and tried to feel us up. He would give us piggyback rides, and as my cousin Evelyn remembers, 'The next thing, you'd feel his hands in your pants.' We also remembered how we had to avoid a cousin's husband's exposed penis and wandering hands. It took a long time for this information to percolate through our ranks, but gradually, as the girl cousins became older and more responsible and more confident and the age differences mattered less, we talked amongst ourselves.

We recalled both good times, like those picnics on the Vaal River, as well as those ugly incidents from our childhood. Vaal means 'dirty.' Our own Vaal River flowed through our happy days on the water!

EARLY SCHOOLDAYS

At the same time that we were learning life's lessons, a more formal education process was taking place. My earliest memories of it date back to kindergarten. It was taught by Mrs Salter and held at the SOE (Sons of England Hall). I remember being in a dancing class and hearing Mrs Salter say to Mrs Sinclair, our other teacher, that I was a vain little thing. Kindergarten was more than just a play school or nursery school; we learnt some basics, and by the time I was old enough to leave, I could read, write, and add. This meant I was ahead for my age and could miss a couple of early school years when I moved on to primary school.

So I was able to start at Selborne School in Standard One. The class was taught by my Auntie Stella. Two of my father's sisters were schoolteachers, and for a while my Auntie Stella and her family lived in my hometown, Vereeniging. My aunts' teaching apparatus was stacked in a large cupboard in their old family home on the corner of Marks Avenue and Leslie Street, the house where my father's old mother sat huddled in the doorway, a babushka on her head. I remember Auntie Stella's class acting out a poem or story about an old woman who had her skirts cut while she was asleep, but I haven't been able to find the work again.

I think of primary school largely in terms of teachers. Mrs Liebenberg, who I had for Standard Three, was a teacher I liked. She made a drawing for my autograph book, which I still have. About that time Princess Elizabeth, now the queen, got married. It was a major event in our lives, and we read about the romance and listened on the radio to the ceremony—there was no television then, of course—and I copied pictures of her wedding dress.

Earlier the same year, in 1947, my friend Dorothy and I went with our mothers on a car trip to a town a few hours away. Cosmos grew on the side of the road as we drove through the Highveld countryside that June. We were going to see the Royal Family in the town where the royal tour was stopping off. I managed to catch a glimpse of the then Queen Elizabeth, consort to George VI, resplendent in powder blue. At school, to mark the visit, we were given commemorative coins nestled in a velvet-like box bearing the king's head. We eagerly followed the affairs of the royals; mostly, the English South Africans did, but in the bigger South African picture, the Afrikaner politicians were setting up the apparatus of apartheid, a platform advocating total separation of the races to prevent the white society eventually being overwhelmed by the black.

There were both English-language and Afrikaans-language schools in our town. In either, one had to learn the other official language. I still have some Afrikaans, quite a lot, though the language has grown and evolved with the rise of *Afrikanerdom*, pride in the Afrikaans language, and culture fostered by the Afrikaans-speaking descendants of the early Dutch settlers. Regardless of language, these schools were all white. During breaks at Selborne, we would loll on the steps outside our classroom. If a white male teacher or student walked by, we would hurriedly sit up and draw our legs together, but a passing black worker went unnoticed.

White Schooldays

We were privileged, being white, but that did not mean we all shared the same level of comfort. If I look at my Standard Six school-class photograph, I see Frank Vorster, wearing an army bomber jacket and short pants—all the boys wore short pants—more than six feet tall, looking like a twenty-year-old and standing out in a class of twelve-year-olds. Kay, a girl who lived round the corner from me, raffled a broken wristwatch for cash. Yvonne's mother baked for a living. Margaret Hardy came to school looking unkempt and unwashed, nose running.

Standard Six was the last year of primary school. Mr Maree was the teacher. He was a stocky man with a bright red face and black hair and moustache. He was very free with the ruler, hitting us across our palms for any misdemeanour. These were called cuts.

We had to make a garment in sewing class that year. My project was a sundress, red-and-white gingham with white edging round the top. The imminent arrival of the school inspector created a panic, and I had to have it completed in time for his visit. My mother had a dressmaker finish it.

South African winters were short, just about two months, in June and July, so central heating was hardly used. Our classrooms were cold, and we worked with our blazers on. I have a painful memory of wool gloves rubbing against chilblains.

Primary school was named after a British politician, Lord Selborne, a high commissioner in South Africa, and governor of the Transvaal and Orange River Colonies in the early 1900s. South Africa was in a period of political change, just beginning in my early school years. *Afrikanerdom* was taking over from things British, but Selborne continued to retain its British connection, at least in name.

Its school uniform was a blue pinafore over a white shirt in summer and in winter, the requisite navy blazer over a navy gym tunic tied by a girdle in the school's colours. The school anthem reflected those colours, and we proudly sang, 'For the blue and gold that our flag unfolds, we'll fight with our might and main.'

HIGH SCHOOL

General Smuts High, like Selborne, was named after a politician, but in this case, a famous South African statesman and military leader who served twice as the country's prime minister. Smuts was a vocal supporter of separation of the races through most of his career, though that would hardly have been a factor in naming the school in 1953.

General Smuts High's uniform was an ugly grey dress with a maroon collar and cuffs. It had to be worn correctly, in or out of the schoolyard, with all the right accessories. In the small-town conservative environment that was Vereeniging, our out-of-school demeanour was watched: proper uniform, no jeans, and no smoking. Detention followed for any offences.

When I got to high school and started high-school subjects, I found that I couldn't do algebra because I couldn't see the figures on the board. So my lifelong love-hate relationship with glasses began.

High school those days was strictly about the fundamentals. The subjects that kids now take for credit—at least here in Canada—would never even have been thought of: family studies, individual family living, media arts, career studies, world religions, and dance! Today's mantra is that every student is unique and that programs should meet individual student's needs. In my day we weren't seen as individuals.

We had to take six subjects to matriculate; that was it, and there was little choice in what they were. I took English and Afrikaans—both of which were compulsory—science, maths, history, and Latin. The alternative to history was typing for those who were not planning to go on to university. The alternative to Latin was art, and I dropped Latin for it, a decision I regret now that I am trying to speak French. Typing properly would also be helpful in today's computer world.

A high school in a small town had its limitations. One of my schoolmates felt high-school French would be an asset and went into the city once a week for lessons. But my narrow high-school education and solid grounding in basics has stood me well as I carry out my daily life, from calculating my gas consumption to managing my finances and adapting recipes.

English grammar was drilled into us and turned me into a grammar policewoman. Even though I break the rules myself and I know that language usage keeps changing, I still cringe when I hear 'very unique.' And Word for Windows and I disagree on the placement of the full stop, aka period, after a title like Mrs or Dr.

I was lucky to have English teachers who encouraged my love of poetry, and I filled my poetry book with poems that struck chords with me. I can still recite old favourites. Lines come back to me: 'Break, break break'...or 'A poem lively as a tree'...and 'A host of golden daffodils.' Afrikaans poems have stayed with me too: *'Maar daardie merk wort grooter,'* an allusion to the defeat of the Boers (Afrikaners) by the Brits and the indelible wound it left, a wound that continued.

But the English language was and has been my great love. I read indefatigably. I had a fantasy—put aside for many years—of being a writer but also, like most teenage girls in those days, of being an air hostess or a dress designer or a model.

The only public performance the school put on that I remember was to celebrate some national anniversary. Those of us who could sing (not me) were dressed up in the colours of the flag and performed a pageant of sorts on an island in Vosloo Park, a riverside venue. Those watching from the bank kept berating kids close by in the audience for eating garlic. It was only long after that I realized the garlic-like smell came from a plant we were trampling or crushing where we sat.

The only school excursion I remember going on was to Pretoria, to the Voortrekker Monument, the huge granite edifice commemorating the Voortrekkers, the Boers, the Afrikaans farmers who travelled north to escape from British control in the Cape. It was also a symbol of growing Afrikaner strength, but at that age in those times, I would not have understood.

In the first three years of high school, we were taught the basics of managing servants. As most white South African families had at least one, this knowledge was felt to be essential to our complete education, even at age thirteen or so. So in Domestic Science, or Dom Sci as we called it, a compulsory course for girls, we learnt about 'keeping servants.' We took down notes dictated by our teacher. I remember a particular point about knowing the last name of a maid so she could be tracked down if she did not show up for work, and she had to be treated with consideration and have her afternoon a week off. If she lived in, her quarters had to be separate, and only she was allowed to live in them; it was illegal to have her husband or child with her.

We illustrated our Dom Sci notebooks lavishly, mainly with cutouts from advertisements in US magazines. For my notes on handling the help, I remember my illustration came from *McCall's* or *Ladies' Home Journal*, and I had captioned it 'The ideal servant.' It was a beaming Aunt Jemima.

TASTE BUDS

For those three years of high school Dom Sci, my partner in cooking ventures was a girl named Shala. We cycled to school together each day and home again; at lunch we swapped our maid Sarah's egg sandwiches for their maid Mary's chicken sandwiches, spoke on the phone for hours, collaborated on homework, and fancied two boys, themselves best friends as well as school prefects, from whom we were delighted to be given 'lines' when we transgressed. Today, I still know 'The quality of mercy is not strained....'

As a cooking duo, Shala and I never attained great culinary skills, but we did manage—no matter how closely we followed the recipe—to end up with more of anything than anyone else.

Sometimes the boys in our class who studied woodwork while we were busy improving our homemaking skills would come in after their lesson and eat our pies and cakes and stews. When they did not, we had to eat them ourselves. I remember my sister coming home green in the face after her finer sensibilities, not to say Jewish upbringing, revolted against eating suet pudding. The Jewish girls did eventually did win a victory of sorts over mixing meat and milk, which our religion didn't allow.

Dom Sci was a course seemingly evolved out of England, the war, rationing, and making do, and it certainly did not encourage waste.

While recipes for some more exotic South African dishes brought in by the Malay slaves, such as *sosatie* and *bobotie*, were included in our Domestic Science textbook, the recipes were heavily English: liver and bacon, mixed grill, steak-and-kidney pudding, stewed steak, sheep's trotters, toad-in-the-hole, and tripe and onions. The book was called *Household Cookery for South Africa*, first published around 1915. I still have my edition, which includes a dietary scale worked out by the Department of Education, which 'has stood the test of time and boys and girls thrive on it....While this scale is for European (white) boys, a very similar one has been worked out for coloured (mulatto) pupils, another for native (black) pupils, and yet another for native labourers.'

My mother would not have known about or observed these scales. Our servants ate what we believed they liked: bread and jam, beef stew, and mealiepap. And our leftovers.

Dom Sci was far behind me once I was at university in the city. I was eating bacon, though it would still be many years later before I ate any other sort of pork; the early Jewish conditioning was hard to get over. But prawns and crayfish were high on my list of favourite foods when I went out to restaurants. We would joke that one could keep a kosher kitchen but have a *traife* (nonkosher) stomach!

I had less contact with day-to-day Jewish life then. I went to the occasional wedding ceremony, and I would get invited for a holiday meal to the home of a relative or fellow student. I remember, I think it was Yom Kippur, the Day of Atonement, when we broke the fast with a meal made entirely of herring dishes!

My Latvian great-great-grandparents

My Latvian great-grandfather

A young Nany

Meyer and Nany in Wiesbaden

Libau Jewish Cemetery after WW2

My mother (foreground) visiting her Latvian relatives

My father at Leslie Street

My father's family in Lithuania waiting to rejoin the men

With my mother and my doll Mavis at Leslie Street

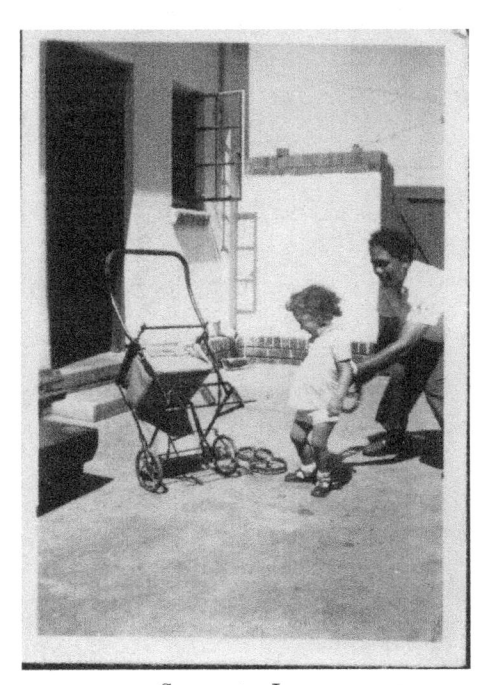

Servants. James

Servants. Sarah

A very young me

Me with Binky-Lou

Pets-Prince

My sister with Smokey

The brown Vauxhall

With a friend in London

My father with friends at Muizenberg Beach

Me in Selborne's winter uniform

Highschool cricket team

House dinner

Rag

Residence initiation

Habonim Camp

Cheder

Shopping with Shala in the city

Estelle's birthday party

A neighbourhood birthday party

Dan's barmitzvah. Shirley and family waiting to go to synagogue

A RELIGIOUS EDUCATION

We were allowed to skip school for major Jewish holidays and to skip Bible-study classes. Having coerced our parents into writing letters to have us excused from studying the New Testament, we retired to the library once a week for a séance of sorts: crouching on the floor with hands on an upturned drinking glass set in a circle of alphabet letters, much like a *planchette,* and willing the glass to move on its own. The dead who were invoked via this method were not always as responsive as our parents, and I remember when a boy named Michael Plit tried to make contact with his deceased uncle, the glass spelled out that he was at a Zionist meeting.

Four afternoons a week we went to *cheder,* classes at the synagogue on the basics of Judaism and the Hebrew language. They were very boring but were mandatory for boys so that they could prepare for their *bar mitzvahs,* their coming-of-age, and girls were obliged to attend. So we went until we were thirteen. I wish I had paid more attention to learning Hebrew. I would have had another language under my belt, other than just the few words I know. I do remember snippets of prayers and can say the blessings for lighting candles and for breaking bread, and I can also recite the four questions, part of the Passover dinner ritual. The *cheder* classes put on annual pageants, and I once wore my blue chenille dressing gown for a part in the story of Esther.

Cheder was taught by Mr Brasch. His daughters, Ali and Heidi, were my classmates and playmates. The family was a later addition to our town. I would be invited occasionally to have Friday-night dinner at their home. After dinner the daughters and the black maids would stand together in front of Mrs Brasch and sing, 'We have a lovely mother.'

The Jewish kids belonged to *Habonim*, a Zionist youth organization. Zionism and the State of Israel were heavily promoted in the Jewish communities. I was not particularly indoctrinated, but my friends and I belonged because in a small town, that's what one did. For me, *Habonim* was more a social activity, though many of the young people who were members of *Habonim* did have strong Zionist sympathies and ended up fighting for Israel or settling there, and it was one of the places, along with the UK and Australia, to which many South African Jews immigrated as an escape from the apartheid regime and in later years, from the country's escalating crime and violence—the diaspora in reverse.

We went to *Habonim* meetings every Sunday morning, and one summer I went away with some of my friends to *Habonim* Camp. We went overnight by train with hundreds of other campers to East London, to a large campground near the ocean. Camp was pretty basic. There were six of us to a tent, which we had to put up ourselves. We slept on bedrolls. If it rained, we got soaked. We had to help with food prep at the large communal kitchen. Showers and toilets were a long walk away. Even the beach for a daily swim was a trek through brush. Singing round the campfire at night was one of the nicer things we did; so was eating the chocolate cake my mother sent, which we cut with a potato peeler. My tentmates and I were hardly being equipped for the rigors of Israeli frontier life!

A JEWISH GIRLHOOD

For us in those childhood years, going to synagogue on the high holidays meant dressing up specially. Every September, prior to *Rosh Hashana*, the Jewish New Year, I would get new party dresses and so did my girlfriends. A seamstress named Mrs Swanepoel made mine. I remember one of blue *Broderie Anglais* and later a blue taffeta pinafore worn over a white blouse with a black-velvet bow at the neck. My friend Dorothy and I went to a neighbour to have our hair curled for these holiday occasions. It was a painful process involving rags from which we emerged with fat, cigar-like ringlets. After I had my hair cut, I set it with pin curls. I had a perm at about age thirteen; straight hair was not considered fashionable. Women usually washed their hair just once a week in those pre-hand dryer days. Vinegar was used as a rinse, supposedly to give it sheen. Egg whites were used for a facial and slices of cucumber to take the bags away from under the eyes.

When I was about thirteen or so, I would go with a friend by bus to the nearby city to buy my New Year finery myself—one year a small, red-velvet hat and a red-leather bag that looked like a lantern;

a few years later, my hat was very grown-up, Garbo-like in orange felt.

Shala, Dawn, and Lorraine were the first girls in our town to have *bat mitzvahs*—coming-of-age ceremonies for girls. *Bat mitzvahs* were becoming popular amongst Jews in South Africa, usually amongst Reform Jews, but even though our synagogue was Orthodox, my friends had a joint ceremony one Saturday morning. In the afternoon we went to each of their houses for a tea-and-cake celebration of sorts.

With just one English-language school in Vereeniging in those years, white English-speaking kids, Jewish and non-Jewish, went to the same school, played together, and went to parties together, and there was some inter-faith dating: Myrna had a relationship with non-Jewish Neil. My friend Shala fancied a school prefect named Barry. Estelle saw someone called Sybrand, and Natalie had a boyfriend called Gus. The Jewish boys may have had non-Jewish girlfriends, but I don't remember any details. Either way, our parents didn't know and certainly would not have approved.

I am still in contact with some of the Jewish girls from Vereeniging. One or two have remained close friends, and when we talk or e-mail, we spark off reminiscences about our shared small-town experiences.

PLAYING FIELDS

I liked to watch sport or listen to it on the radio but not to participate. I managed to get out of gym and playing sports almost all of my schooldays. My mother wrote the excuses.

There were not many sports that girls played at our school other than rounders, a form of baseball. The boys played cricket, soccer, and rugby. I still have the team photographs. It was compulsory for the girls to go to see the boys play. In my final year of high school, we went to watch the British Lions rugby team train. They were training at a field in our town, Vereeniging, during a visit to South Africa. I developed a crush on the tall, red-headed Tony O'Reilly. He later became one of Ireland's richest businessmen, married to a Greek heiress, a far cry from playing on a local field in a small South African town and signing a gawking teenager's autograph book.

It was perhaps a misplaced belief on the part of our mothers, but we were not allowed to go to the swimming pool until the first rains of spring had fallen. Then, during the long hot summers, we went almost every afternoon after school. The local pool was next door to the park where, as very small children, we went on the swings and the slide, and paddled in the wading pool. I learnt to swim but never to dive. The teacher was Danish, an ex-Olympian. Drying off after a lesson or cavorting with my friends in the shallow end would be followed by the pleasure of lying facedown on my towel with the sun on my back.

I went with my friend Estelle to her golf lessons at our local country club. The attraction was the local pro, not the game itself, and I watched him holding her shoulders as he taught her how to swing. My mother wanted me to play tennis; like bridge, there would always be a need for someone to be a fourth, but I got out of that, too. My parents were middle-aged when they had me; they didn't play outdoor games with me, so lobbing a ball wasn't in my comfort zone.

My father was not a sports fan, though one year he had somehow got tickets to a big international rugby match in the nearby city and took me. I got into trouble because I missed some must-attend school event, a fund-raiser I think. I can remember my father going with friends to his first and only boxing match, a big marquee number with expensive tickets. I think one of the fighters was Jewish. There was a knockout in the first round, and it was all over in minutes.

I sometimes went with my father to the horse races when I was old enough, and I would dress up to go. It still seemed quite glamorous then. A race called the Durban July was the big event of the year, away in the coast city of Durban, and we would listen to its broadcast, still on the radio, of course, in those days. Tiger Wright was a famous jockey who rode in it and in other big races, and we would shout encouragingly, 'Ride 'im, Tiger.' These days there is another famous Tiger in the sports world, and when I watch him play golf, I urge him on and say, 'Ride 'im, Tiger.'

My mother tried lawn bowls, under pressure from her friends, and went off to join them in her white dress and white Panama hat. But she was not sports inclined and gave it up after a few months.

Like me, she preferred to stay home and read. The closest I came to lawn bowls was wearing a white bowling dress under my academic gown for formal events at university.

As teenagers in Vereeniging, we would listen to the cricket test matches on the radio, hearing phrases like 'a small cloud drifts over the pitch and casts its shadow,' and we would telephone each other about the scores. Later, as a university student, my cousin Isador got me tickets to cricket matches, and my friend Shala and I would sit up in the stands at the Wanderers Grounds each day of the three- or-four-day event, enjoying the sun and eating hot dogs and drinking Cokes.

All these sports events were for whites only; the players were white, and so were the spectators, and we gave no thought to their black counterparts. South Africa was a sports-mad nation, and so the international sports community banned South Africa's participation, to pressure the government to change its apartheid policy, but it took several decades and Mandela's release for sport to become integrated and to see blacks and whites together on a sports field singing together the anthem 'nKosi Sikelel' iAfrika.'

Lord Bless Africa!

EXTRACURRICULAR

Mothers from a similar milieu were very keen on giving us whatever extracurricular opportunities were available. Activities included dressmaking with Mrs Conradie, elocution with one of the Gavshon daughters, flower arranging with Miss Hosford, and art with Mrs Prentiss. Mrs Miller, a friend of my mother's, gave us a few cooking lessons, but all I learnt from her was how to soften butter and shred lettuce. At first-aid classes, I learnt to make a bed with tight 'hospital corners.' Fitted sheets were decades away.

I went as a spectator to *eisteddfod*s (a Welsh festival of literature, music and performance) in the city to see my friends perform; they were there for dancing, not speech or singing. I was never good enough to compete, though I did go to dance classes. A ballet teacher from the city, Natalie Stern, came to teach us once a week. The more gifted went to lessons in the city. One of these, a year ahead of me in school, was Juliet Prowse. We knew her then as Juliet Polte; Polte was her step-father's surname. He was a nearby building-contractor client of my father's.

'I never graduated from college,' Juliet once said, 'because I became so interested in dancing that when I was sixteen, I quit to study with the ballet teacher Marjorie Sturman in Johannesburg.' Marjorie Sturman's troupe would visit our town and put on a show on an island in Vosloo Park, a riverside venue, performing well-known classical ballets. Juliet would have been one of the leads.

Juliet left South Africa for London to try to get into the Royal Ballet but was too tall. She joined the London Palladium, went to Paris, later became a movie actress, and was involved with Frank Sinatra. I continued to follow her career, and I tried unsuccessfully to see her backstage when she performed in Toronto many years later.

We took tap-dancing lessons with Russell Meister, a local teacher. We wore red Capezio tap shoes, tied with bows on top. When you loosened the taps, they made a tinkling sound as one moved. I went to tap awhile. My friend Dorothy lasted longer. I can see her in a little green-and-white frilly costume performing a number called 'An Apple for the Teacher,' possibly to the Bing Crosby tune, I am not sure. Now and then, if the mood is right and the tune is right, I 'Shuffle Off to Buffalo,' shuffling being one of the only two steps that ever stuck. The Meisters lived across the street from Dorothy and up the street from me. Russell Meister's sister Rosalie was at school with us and wore a crinoline under her grey uniform. The brother-and-sister duo was well known on the competitive Latin dance circuit. My friend Shala took Spanish dancing. I loaned her a red Spanish shawl that had been my grandmother's for a performance. It was in an old trunk together with my mother's evening dresses from long before her marriage: one was turquoise silk patterned with little pink roses and trimmed with wide bands of silver lace, the other almost diaphanous in shades of gold. We would dress up in these.

I still have the shawl, shades of red with a long fringe. It may have been draped over my grandmother's piano. We had a piano in our Leslie Street house, but my mother gave or returned the piano to her stepsisters. I used to look at the sheet music that was left behind, pieces like 'In a Chinese Temple Garden' that my mother would have played. When we moved to Marks Avenue, I was signed up for piano lessons with Mrs Rothman, round the corner. I went to my aunt's to practice, as my mother had given our piano away. Mrs Rothman hit me over the hands when I played a wrong note. My music career was soon over.

When we were a bit older, we went to ballroom dancing classes, the girls joined by some of the boys from our crowd. The main high-school social activity was a dance held at the Sons of England Hall. My Afrikaans teacher danced with me and asked in Afrikaans if I liked it when he held me close. The Matric Farewell, also a dance, was held for the graduating class. Unlike today's proms, one didn't go with a date, get a corsage, and get picked up by limo. We wore our ballerina dresses—mine was strapless white tulle—and went solo to the nearby town hall and hoped to be asked to dance!

HIGHER EDUCATION

With high school over, we eagerly awaited our matric exam results. If we had the right marks to qualify for university, the next few months were filled with preparations—registering, getting into a residence, getting the right clothes, and choosing the course to follow. I was only sixteen when I finished high school—the result of the grades I skipped as a young child—when these decisions were being made. Compared to the sixteen-year-olds I know today, I think I was quite mature for my age when I left home for the University of the Witwatersrand in the nearby city of Johannesburg, but that's hindsight.

There was nothing to keep young people in Vereeniging with its two cinemas and one main street. There were the industries—coal, steel, and so on—and some of my classmates stayed on to work in them. But many of us left. For a nice middle-class Jewish girl like me, going to university and getting a BA and a husband was the desired path, and I followed it.

What was a university education like? I took an arts degree; that's what young women took who were not going into professions like physiotherapy. There was little in my courses that captured the imagination, at least for me. At an undergraduate level, we were not encouraged to challenge or question. I went to my classes, did my assignments, got a Bachelor of Arts degree, and followed it with one of the few options open to girls at that time, such as teaching or librarianship. I did the latter.

Some teachers stood out. Lexie Longmore, whose fiancé was killed in the war, took us on an anthropology field trip to Swaziland, where we spent a lot of time drinking Tom Collinses at the pool of the Swazi Inn. Hazel Mews's name describes her—British with braids wound around the top of her head. She taught Library Science. Zoe Girling was a good English teacher, but we only had her for a few months. She and her husband left the country, like so many South African academics who could not tolerate the apartheid system. One day quite a few years later, I was at a farmer's market in Toronto. I looked up, and there was Zoe checking out the tomatoes.

I wanted to wear the university's blazer in stripes of blue, white, and yellow, so I did all the chores—selling the university magazine and so on—to earn the necessary points. I did knit a cardigan in the university colours, which I wore to the big rugby matches against our main rival, the Afrikaans University of Pretoria.

There were very few black students at the university then, though they were still allowed to go at that time. I recall only two black women in all my classes. The government policy for separate nonwhite education was beginning to take place during my university days.

Looking back, I see now that I was amongst the privileged, that I was living and learning in a parallel universe, and that millions of black kids were denied my kind of education. If only they had been allowed the same opportunities, South Africa would be a very different country.

GENERATION GAP

I went to my university reunion the other evening. It was one of the few alumni reunions held in Toronto by the University of the Witwatersrand, familiarly known as Wits. I think one did take place many years ago, on a snowy January evening in the northern suburbs of the city, where most expat South Africans have settled. I did not get to it, given the weather and my downtown location. Now, in 2013, I was curious to see who would be attending. There are apparently over five hundred of us in this city, known ex–South Africans who attended Wits. The event was held in a meeting room on the thirty-fourth floor of a local law firm, arranged by one of the lawyers, an ex–South African Wits alumnus like me.

The reason for the reunion was obviously to raise funds. Toronto was one of several North American cities visited by the organizers. Their presentation was about the university today, so much larger and spread out than in my time, over fifty years ago. They were looking for monies to move it into the top tier of academic institutions, despite its not-insignificant achievements over the years.

There were about sixty attendees. Only a handful was nonwhite. The group was largely male, many of them lawyers and doctors, and the average age was over sixty. I wondered about this demographic: Is it because older people value their past? Or reach back into their past as they grow older? Or have more time as they retire? Or because those of us who attended the event have happy memories of a special time under the South African sun?

Through an online Wits alumni discussion group that I joined a few years ago through LinkedIn, I encountered Kevin. We had interests in common, and when we discovered we both lived in Toronto, we arranged to meet for coffee. Kevin is a young black man with impressive qualifications, including, amongst others, a BA Honours Degree from Wits.

He had come to Canada after meeting in Johannesburg—and later marrying—a Canadian woman who had come to study at Wits. At the time he and I got together, he was looking for work as he was just finishing up some of his Toronto studies. I was able to help him get a job, and that has translated into many Sunday-morning coffees in my neighbourhood. He and his wife have recently bought a condo and had a baby boy.

Kevin is a child of the black townships, born in the early 1980s, in the apartheid era. His mother was a domestic and his father a gardener. As a teenager, he had gone looking for work in a white neighbourhood. A couple who knew his father decided to help him, later taking him in and putting him through high school and university. By the time he was ready to attend university, the apartheid government's policy of separate education for the races had fallen away. With Mandela in power, it was a time when freedom of education was available in principle for all.

Would someone like Kevin attend the reunion? Did he feel ties to the university and his time there? Being of a younger generation with a different attitude to events and associations such as these, did he have anything in common? He is certainly of a black generation

White Schooldays

who would have a very different set of memories of university life, of South African life in general, and of his life in particular.

I contrast our university experiences, looking at mine of the 1950s. I was a young white woman mixing with other whites, and the opportunity and the inclination to do otherwise was not in my consciousness. I became aware of the apartheid government's deplorable education policies as a Wits student but was not an active protester. A few of my friends from the all-white classrooms and the all-white residence where I lived are still my friends today. Like most of the attendees at the reunion, we are a homogeneous bunch. Fifty years later we would all fit in to the reunion and other events like it.

The invitation was targeted at those who could contribute financially. Kevin's generation might not be ready to respond to this sort of corporate approach or have the wherewithal to donate, and many of his fellow students now living in Canada would be under the alumni radar, not feeling a bond to their alma mater or the need to keep the contact. Few of his peers would be present, those attending would have a different shared experience, and there might be a political or social disconnect. The older alumni may have been politically active in their day and would of course be politically aware and politically correct, but they emerged from a different political and cultural environment and from a university life that did not have the diversity of the Wits of today, the university Kevin attended.

There are tens of millions of black South Africans who have not been fortunate enough to have Kevin's opportunities, who will never have an invitation to a reunion, and whose chances have been wasted by the years of an oppressive regime. But fifty years from now, Kevin and his peers may think back to their school years and may want to accept an invitation to a reunion, as they look back over the decades and at what education meant to them; they were lucky enough to have been able to benefit from it in the emerging and changing fabric of the new South Africa.

In the meantime, as an alumnus, I continue to get my copy of the *Wits Review*, and so I get to keep up with the changing campus. I have found out about old friends and colleagues from my university years. In the last few months, there have been two obituaries and one tribute! I don't feel emotional reading them; they just take me back in time to my young self, a reminder of opportunities I took for granted.

RESIDENCE

There were few accommodation options then for young women students when I went to university in the city, and so I signed up for the university's only women's residence. I joined the 150 or so all-white women from all over southern Africa—from Mozambique, the Rhodesias, and South West Africa, as those countries were named in those days. I am writing about the 1950s.

The life in a university residence in those times may not be of any great interest today, but those privileged years represent a small slice of a social history, the South Africa of those times in a microcosm.

The residence, Lady Isabel Dalrymple House, commonly called Sunnyside, was a traditional residence exclusively for young women students from out of town. It was set in well-manicured grounds on the campus, a three-story white building with a small parking area in front. It backed onto one of the main city thoroughfares, Empire Road, where in the '50s we could see women of the Black Sash—a nonviolent white women's resistance organization—standing on its sidewalks in silent vigil to protest the apartheid government's moves to set up a separate school system for nonwhites, legislation, which was extended to include universities during my time as a student.

But in February of 1957, young and politically unsophisticated, I arrived from Vereeniging, only thirty-six miles away, by car with my mother and my suitcases, eiderdown, radio, and other bits and pieces for my new life.

I had no sooner unpacked when I was summoned to the front door. There was no intercom system then or phones in the rooms. Maids (black) did door duty in the daytime, and first-year students did it on a rotation basis nights and weekends. You were fetched to the door to meet with your visitor or date. If the person was a male, he never got beyond reception.

One of the second-year guys from my hometown had come to say hello and to check out the new crop of arrivals. He came from the men's residence a few hundred yards away. In those first months, we shared several activities with the men's residence: an 'exchange' dance, when we trooped over to be selected by the new men as dinner partners, a very demeaning experience, particularly if you were one of the last to be chosen. We also got together with the men for a concert of sorts. I remember performing to 'Green Door.' Before all of this though, we had initiation—dressing up in weird clothing and marching in pairs with the freshmen to something called Fresher's Flick. The women were called Freshettes.

Accommodation was handed out based on academic success. I did well in high school, and so I had a room of my own. There was no such thing as en suite. Bathrooms, showers, and toilets were down the hall. Rooms were minimal though quite pleasant. Today's dorms have minifridges and microwaves and television sets and other accoutrements. In those days South Africa did not even have television! The rooms were cleaned by the maids, and they changed the linen every week. The maids were under the supervision of the matrons (white), who took care of the daily running of the place.

White Schooldays

We ate in a communal dining room. Breakfast and lunch were casual, but dinner started on time, and we wore black academic gowns and for formal occasions, a white dress under the gown. Food was institutional but not horrible. Dinner could be slices of grey roast meat. Leftover cheese ended up as Welsh rarebit. We had tea in a common room every afternoon with nice cake or cookies. There was a senior common room and a junior common room. The university commissary was close by, too. In fourth year we often picnicked in the garden rather than go in to dinner. We would walk up the hill to pick up sausages and other goodies from a German deli or from a café on the edge of the campus. And my mother sent her special cookies and chocolate cake regularly.

Being in residence made attending early morning classes easier. We were right there on the campus. We rolled up our pyjama pants under a coat, and off we went. The swimming pool was almost at the door, too, for an afternoon's reading in the sun. And for meeting guys.

In our first few months in residence, lectures were organized for us, some on sex education. There were still young women who needed to know where babies came from. South Africa was very conservative and straitlaced. Many of us came from small towns or rural communities and several from convent schools. A first-year colleague from Mozambique was not allowed to go out at night without a chaperone. We gossiped a lot, usually late at night in one or another's room, smoking and eating my mother's goodies. Some of us continued long-distance relationships with boyfriends from home; many others paired up quickly with men from the student body. We never let on if we 'did it.' Not in those days. Abortion gossip circulated that someone had tried it with a knitting needle. And one of us got pregnant and left to have a baby.

Our residence had its own float for Rag, an annual fund-raising event that no longer exists. We decorated trucks for a carnival-like procession through the city—much like the Macy's Christmas

Parade—and collected money from the people watching on the streets. One float was for the Rag Queen and her princesses. One of the princesses from my time almost became the wife of a US president many years later had John Kerry only won, but at least she became the wife of a secretary of state.

Our residence phone system was basic. There was a bank of public phones, four, I think. They were manned by the maids during the day and by first-year students the rest of the time, who, like the front-door monitors, fetched us to the phone. The corridors were long and spread out, and there were no elevators, so by the time one reached the phone, the caller might be long gone.

We had house dances twice a year to which one invited a date. The invitation process of asking or receiving a reply was stressful, particularly given the unreliability of the phone system! Bedrooms at the front of the building were set aside for small groups of two or three couples, and dancing took place in the dining room. Punch (nonalcoholic) was made in the matrons' bathtub. One year a couple of women came together, one dressed in a man's suit. It was quite the talk!

There was a curfew system. We had to be in by eight p.m. most nights and could only be out later a certain number of nights per week, two I think in first year. Saturday night was the big going-out night. The place was abuzz with women in curlers who were ironing, showering, and getting ready for a date or a party. To be in on a Saturday night was depressing, almost demeaning. In those days, women did not go out together at night, to a movie or a restaurant. It wasn't the danger factor, like today; it was just not done. Going-out nights required asking for permission during set office hours from the dean or the assistant dean. One signed in and out, and being late was a serious offence. As we progressed through the years towards a degree, the rules became much more flexible, just as the choice of rooms got better.

Friendships were strong and would stand through the years that followed. Romance was rife, and engagements happened. Many of us stayed until we graduated. Then we went on to new lives, to marriage, or to chosen careers, and many of us went to other countries with awakened consciences as we grew up and experienced the real world out there!

FRIENDSHIP

I have lost touch with most of my university friends, but for some reason I can recite the birthdays of girls with whom I grew up in Vereeniging so many decades ago: Dorothy, February 14; Jacky, February 24; Dawn, March 4; Elaine, March 8; Carol, April 6; Lorraine in May; Shala in August; in September, the other Jacky, Brenda, and Myrna.

Carol was probably my first real friend. It's all so long ago. She lived in an apartment with her mother not too far from our house on Leslie Street and came to play in our living room. We also played in her aunt's garden in a sandpile, making tunnels and sending a golf ball down them.

Carol's mother was the cashier at one of our two local cinemas, the Metro Bioscope, as we called a cinema in those days, and we would get in for free. One year Carol and I ended up with the same summer dresses. Our mothers had taken us shopping separately to the city. Our dresses were green. This was unusual for me, as my mother was superstitious and never bought anything green. After the war, we had to wait longer than necessary for a car, waiting for one that wasn't green. Even today I own very little that's green. It's not planned or conscious. Carol was sent away to boarding school, got married not that long after graduating, and then divorced. And took up golf. I've lost touch with her, but I know this because the Vereeniging strands of our lives still interconnect: Carol's daughter makes Dorothy's travel arrangements.

Dorothy and I shared so many experiences, but there was a huge gap in our relationship after I went abroad. Dorothy married Richard and had four children and a good life until he dropped dead at the dinner table. It was after his death that Dorothy and I reconnected and have become extremely good friends, as though no time has passed. She lives in a small South African town, has been a literacy teacher to needy blacks, and keeps busy in the small Jewish community. She has remarried and once wrote to me that she had butterflies in her stomach in anticipation of her new beau's visit. It gave me such pleasure to know that she was given another stab at romance and that these feelings were still possible, no matter one's age. She keeps in touch with some of the old Vereeniging gang, and I get the news about them from her.

Some have died, like Estelle. Estelle was the only child of a couple who ran the Royal Hotel. The Royal is the hotel my parents stayed at when they were first married, an older hotel like the National where our schoolmates, Jeff and his brother, lived with their widowed mother. The Hilton, which Dorothy's husband Richard managed, was a much later addition. I have photographs of Estelle with her Pekinese, Binky Lou, on the balcony of the Royal Hotel. I always enjoyed eating meals in the Royal's dining room with the white-linen tablecloths and napkins. We would play in the family's suite; Estelle had cupboards full of toys. We would send requests to the pop-music station in Mozambique, mailing them in envelopes we coloured red, so they would stand out. None of our requests ever got selected, though. We painted our nails green and blue with samples from Cutler's pharmacy. We went to try on grown-up shoes

White Schooldays

at Daddaby's, a general store on our main street, owned by Asians. I saw a pair at Daddaby's that I fell madly in love with, a pair of high-heeled, open-toed, sling-back navy shoes with white trim. I took them home on approval, or appro, as we called it. My mother said absolutely not—I was too young.

I only bring up this small incident because, when the South African government of those apartheid years introduced the Group Areas Act a few years later, Daddaby's was forced to move away from downtown to an Asian-only area. Though Estelle and I were not politically aware, it was a sign—young as we were—of the coming inequities of a racially divided society.

Estelle, like Carol, was sent off to boarding school, to Bloemfontein. I went with her and her parents when she went to register. We took off with some boys I knew, leaving her parents worried about our absence. We hadn't bothered to warn them. One day in Vereeniging, we saw an attractive boy on the main street, a newcomer; we knew almost everyone else. We brought him into our social circle. He is in the photograph I have of Estelle's fifteenth or sixteenth birthday party in 1954, a photograph that includes almost everyone about whom I am writing.

Jacky's father was a butcher, and we ate steaks at her house, learning the best way to prepare them. Jacky got married very young. I went to her afternoon wedding in the garden of her relatives in a Vereeniging suburb. I saw her once, on an early trip back to South Africa. She was already a widow, a young widow. She told me that what she missed most was not having anyone with whom to go out for a drink. Women just didn't go out on their own or with women friends in those days. I heard from Dorothy that Jacky died recently.

Jeanette hasn't figured very much in my stories, perhaps because her family came to Vereeniging when we were already in high school. My main memory of Jeanette is going with her and her boyfriend Jack to dances at the Riviera Hotel on Saturday nights. I went with Jack's friend, whose name I can't recall. The boys, young men really, came all the way from a town called Krugersdorp to take us out. Jeanette married Jack not too long after but is now widowed, and I have heard via the Vereeniging network that she is living in a retirement complex.

Most of my childhood friends stayed on in South Africa, but I have remained in contact with some of them and with one or two who left. We correspond by e-mail. I send my usual birthday wishes to them. Friends remember birthdays and wish each other 'many happy returns.'

PARTY POLITICS

The first birthday party I can remember was my own. It was my sixth birthday, just a few days after my sister was born, and I fell into a nest of red ants and had to be carted off into a bathtub. Birthday parties in those days were quite simple, not the elaborate events they can be today, with entertainers and so on. They took place in the afternoon; we arrived in party clothes, bringing gifts, and played games until it was time to sit round a table laden with all sorts of sweet things: pink-and-white meringues pressed together with whipped cream and of course, a birthday cake layered with whipped cream or strawberry jam, 'Happy Birthday' scrolled on top, and little candles—five, six, or seven, for whatever the age being celebrated—standing up in pink or blue rosettes in the frosting. After the birthday boy or girl blew out the candles with one big whoosh and made the obligatory secret wish, we sang 'Happy Birthday to You.' Presents were opened, and then games continued until a parent came to collect his or her offspring.

Growing up in a small town, we all knew each other, and usually the same group of kids circulated from birthday party to birthday party. I remember making a huge fuss about the invitation from Lorraine, not wanting to go, because we were going to be seated boy-girl-boy-girl. How we change! At another birthday party, we used plastic straws for the first time and had to turn them in for reuse.

As we grew older, we started having evening parties, perhaps for a birthday or just because. The first of these that I went to was at my friend Dorothy's house. It was actually her older brother's party, but she and I made sure we were included. I wore a blue plaid skirt and a pink twinset decorated with a blue Fair Isle pattern. And I probably wore ankle socks! The fight with our mothers about wearing mascara was soon to begin.

My age group held some parties of our own. Our crowd mostly included those of us who went to the same high school, those of us who were around until we went off to university or wherever. During the winter and summer holidays, the kids who had been sent off to boarding school joined our ranks. We gathered at someone's house, danced to Frank Sinatra or Nat King Cole, and as the music slowed and the lights dimmed, made out, or some of us did. We called it smooching.

Sometimes a carload of guys drove in from the nearby city, and that really made the girls' night. The visit didn't get reversed very often. My parents did not drive, but they let our black driver take me and some friends to a party in the city occasionally, perhaps to a holiday reunion. My mother was against a party I wanted to have when I must have been twelve or thirteen, but I plotted with friends, and they called my mother and told her they were planning a surprise party for me. She was flattered, and the party happened, spilling out into our back garden, behind the servant's quarters. I remember the dress I wore: white with sprigs of pink flowers, a sweetheart neck edged with pink, and a gathered skirt with a tulle underlay.

White Schooldays

We were all, of course, white. This was in the apartheid era. The crowd was mixed Jewish and non-Jewish, the result of being juxtaposed in a small town. Jewish-only events were associated with bar mitzvahs. We were all English-speaking. The Afrikaans-speaking kids who went to the Afrikaans medium school were never part of our scene.

My friend Estelle's sixteenth birthday is the last of those parties from my high school years that I can clearly recall. Her parents managed the Royal Hotel, and so she was able to have a large crowd in the dining room, which had been cleared for it. I have the photograph of us all there, with our names written on the back, though I can still identify almost everyone. I go through it and see Peter who died young, Warren who committed suicide, and also Jeffrey. Michael and Zalman became doctors; only Michael has outlived Zalman. Jackie was widowed young, Carol divorced young, and there are my oldest friends, Dorothy and Shala. Estelle herself, a beautiful young woman, whose life played out tragically, apparently died of an overdose. And many of the others, like me, left the country during the unhappy apartheid years.

DAN'S BAR MITZVAH

After I left South Africa, I seldom went back. But one of the occasions I did go home, as I call South Africa even after all these years away, was for my nephew Dan's bar mitzvah. It was still during those apartheid years. And just like the celebrations of my youth, the religious ceremony and luncheon reception was followed by an evening party for Dan's friends.

Shirley, the black maid who had worked for my sister since my nephew was born and who had looked after him through thirteen years, summoned her son Stephen to the event, in his case from the farm in Bopututswana where he lived with his grandparents. All dressed up, he looked like a city boy, even though in those days he was not allowed by law to live there with his mother. The two of them sat in the synagogue, two sole black figures in the white congregation, proudly listening to my nephew read his portion of the service.

In the early evening, Dan's friends started arriving. With religion and family served, this was their time to celebrate. Their formal synagogue clothes off, they came in their running shoes and

T-shirts for hot dogs and hamburgers and to rock with the DJ under the strobe lights of the instant teenage party package.

The grown-ups continued to drink outside in a desultory fashion, the communion of the evening Scotch. At one time I went indoors for some more ice. I looked into the room where the youngsters were dancing, nice middle-class kids having a good time. Also watching them was the black boy Stephen, still all smartly dressed in the clothes specially bought for today, a boy the same age as the rest but not so much as even noticed by them as he stood in the shadows, a boy as bright as the rest, but it would never even have occurred to them to include him. For him, did he feel left out? Would it ever even cross his mind, or would he even dare to think in those days that he could be one of them? As for me, I had had a few drinks, and I stood helplessly in the doorway watching him watch the others.

HOME COOKING

Food for festive occasions—bar mitzvahs, weddings, and the like—was quite elaborate, but the food we ate at home was quite plain, usually meat and potatoes. My mother would phone the butcher and place an order for the week's meat: liver, lamb chops, steak, and chicken, and each week we would eat these in rotation. She would also order something called servants' meat, stew of some sort, I think. Friday nights we usually had fried fish. We weren't catholic, of course, but fish on Friday nights was common amongst Jewish families. Fruit salad was a regular dessert. Fresh fruit was plentiful from the weekly farmer's market or from roadside stands. We took for granted baskets of guavas, lychees, papaws, granadillas, mangoes, peaches, and apricots. These names seem so exotic as I write them, but the fruits were commonplace. Greens were more limited. We only knew one kind of lettuce, iceberg, and asparagus was white and came out of a can. Meals were prepared by our black cook, but my mother did the baking. Her repertoire was chocolate cake, cookies—biscuits we called them—and an apple tart, but for the Jewish holidays, she would make *kneidlach* or *perogen*, or bake her *boolkes,* sweet buns.

She often had friends in for either morning or afternoon tea and always served something she had baked. Home baking was de rigueur in her circle. Each woman had a specialty. My mother would lay the table with a tea cloth, her good china tea service, and the comestibles, and then cover it all with a net to keep the flies off. I embroidered quite a few of these nets as well as doilies, tray cloths, tea cloths, tablecloths, and dressing-table sets to be sold at Jewish charity bazaars. My grandmother had been a great embroiderer; one couldn't tell the back from the front on her work. That was what I was supposed to aim for.

The ladies sat round the table, and tea was poured from a silver teapot, with the requisite hot-water jug for seconds. We drank a lot of tea, early morning with breakfast, at ten a.m., after lunch, in the afternoon, after dinner, and sometimes before bed. It was often my job to make the tea, and I learnt to make it properly, warming the teapot and the cups. We put the milk in first, though in North America, it seems to be the other way around.

Recipes of some of the cakes and cookies that my mother made have come down through the decades with me. I keep my collection of recipes in a 6Ð x 8Ð card file, an accumulation of years of clipping and pasting. I see the recipe for my mother's chocolate cake in her distinctive hand, and her recipe for apricot-jam pudding, too. I have South African cookbooks, old ones like my high-school cookbook, and one put out by a Jewish charity. I also have new ones celebrating the awakening tastes of a less-prejudiced continent. I cook some South African dishes out of the old books. I make them because they are delicious. And yes, they remind me of South Africa. I am happy that I am able to create some of these tastes in my kitchen but also that I can savour the tastes of my youth when I close my eyes. These are part of my DNA. They represent something special that I have brought with me to my adopted country.

LOCAL TASTES

◆

All expats like me probably remember *koeksisters, boerewors, sosaties, biltong,* and *melktert*, all foodstuffs still hugely popular in South Africa and the things I ask for when I go back.

Koeksisters are sugar-filled confections much like baklava. They are complicated to make, though my friend Shala and I did try once or twice. My mother ordered them from Mrs Paton, a local woman who baked for a living. Her plump, red-headed, freckled daughter Yvonne was at school with me. In a small town, we all knew each other. My mother didn't drive, so Daniel, our black driver, would take her to pick up the goodies on a Friday afternoon.

Boerwors, or farmer's sausage, is one of the mainstays of the *braai,* the barbecue, one of South Africa's favourite social events; so are *sosaties,* cubes of lamb marinated in a curry-and-onion sauce and then threaded onto skewers and grilled.

Biltong is not really a food; it's dried meat like pemmican. My mother came from a sheep-farming community in the Karoo and would occasionally get sent a parcel of *biltong,* sheep, or *springbok*. We would chew on a whole stick or slice it and even grate it and have it on our sandwiches for school lunch. It would be spread on *schmaltz*, chicken fat, not butter, because as Jews we did not mix meat and milk.

I would meet my girlfriends every Saturday morning in my early teens, and we would go off for tea. It was the age of big skirts, and I wore a hooped petticoat under mine or otherwise a crinoline so heavily starched that the starch flaked off like snow as I walked. We would go to a tearoom upstairs on our main street and order *melktert*, a custard-filled pie shell with a distinct flavour. Later, the Penguin Milk Bar opened, and that became our Saturday destination for Coke floats or milk shakes or sundaes. We went to school with the owner's daughters, one of whom was called Lynn, and we visited their apartment, intrigued by the owner's wife who seemed so much younger and more attractive than our mothers.

Pannekoek, very thin crepes served with sugar and cinnamon, have always felt very South African to me. They were often sold at Saturday-morning church bazaars at our town hall. I have had many crepes since, but none have equalled the Afrikaner version. *Vetkoek* was another Afrikaner specialty, pieces of dough deep fried in fat and sprinkled with sugar or jam. We weren't counting calories in those days.

South Africa had a large Asian population, descendants of the indentured labourers brought from India to work on the sugar plantations, so curries were common. We ate them at home quite often. On holiday in Durban, with its big Indian population, we would visit the Indian Market to buy doll's furniture made from rattan but also to savour the display of exotic spices and curry powders like Mother-in-law's tongue, a really hot one. When I left home to live in the city, my friends and I would often eat at neighbourhood Indian restaurants, the hot curries served with a tray of garnishes like peanuts, coconut, tomatoes, cucumber, and so on. We would also pick up Indian takeout; it had to be takeout, as certain areas were declared out-of-bounds to us, this being the era of separation of the races, and Indians being one of those races.

Chinese food was not very common at that time. The Chinese population in South Africa was not large. In Vereeniging, where I grew up as a child, the mythology was that the Chinese ate cats and dogs. The few Chinese restaurants in the city served the food banquet-style, one dish following the other, not all at once, as restaurants tend to do these days.

We didn't have real restaurants in my hometown, Vereeniging, in those days. What we had were cafés, establishments almost always owned by Greeks. There was usually a row of booths for meals in the back. A mixed grill or a monkey-gland steak (steak served with a spicy sauce) were the most popular items, and Coke floats or milkshakes were the popular drinks. There was a counter for candy and cigarettes in the front. Phillip's Café was in a building owned by my father's family. The Phillips brothers were Cypriots, not Greeks, but the distinction wasn't one we made. When my mother ran out of something after shopping hours, like butter, she would ask George or Chris to send it over. It was a small town, and nothing was far away.

We had fish-and-chips shops. We'd stop off on our way home from school and buy chips, arguing after we'd eaten them about who got to lick the vinegar-and-salt-infused paper. Tearing it in half was one solution. We also stopped off after school at a confectioner's to buy chocolate mice. A local bakery here in Toronto makes them occasionally, and I always buy them when I see them; they take me back to my childhood and to the tastes and treats I enjoyed.

Sometimes in the afternoon after school, I would cut myself a hunk of what we knew as sweet-milk cheese, probably Edam. It was the only cheese we ever had.

My family never served wine with meals, and I don't recall that any of my friends' families did. I don't know if it was cultural or if it was because we were in a backwoods area that was not very sophisticated. My father had a Scotch every evening before dinner. The maid would bring him a tray with the bottle, the glass, the water, and the ice. One evening when I was about sixteen, he asked her to bring a glass for me. He said that if I was going to drink, it shouldn't be behind his back, and if I was going to drink, it should be Scotch; it was pure. Scotch is still my drink, though I did have lapses in my youth for brandy-and-Coke, ginger squares, and other mixes designed to cause a hangover.

I went with my father every now and then to visit a customer's farm alongside the river, a half-hour's drive away. We always left the farm with a bag of freshly picked corn. We boiled and ate it right away. The next morning we toasted the leftover cobs in the coal stove, which heated water for our house. It was white corn. Peaches and cream hadn't come to South Africa. There were other kinds of corn: *samp* or *stampkoring*, literally 'pounded' corn, was one, also the unfortunately named kafir corn, or sorghum. We grew a special kind in our backyard for making popcorn. The name for corn was *mealies*. *Mealiepap* was—and still is—the staple food for many black South Africans. It's really polenta and is usually eaten with stewed meat. We liked it when the servants made *stywe mealiepap*, which was *mealiemeal* cooked thick and stiff so that it formed a crust on the bottom of the pan, which was quite delicious.

Many South Africans now live in Toronto, having come here in the apartheid years, or more recently, because of the growing crime and violence. Stores selling South African foodstuffs have sprung up in the northern suburbs where most South Africans have settled. When I found out about these, I made a special trip to pick up *snoek* (smoked fish), *kingclip* (also a fish), Anchovette paste, Cola Tonic, Mrs Ball's Chutney, Ouma Rusks, *mealiemeal*, and even *boerewors*. But I found Winnipeg goldeye is nicer than *snoek*, and many other local Canadian products are better than their South African counterparts. Memory and reality don't always jibe.

OUTSIDE INFLUENCES

Cycling, in my early Vereeniging years, was the main means of getting around our small town. Our bicycles were either black Rudges or Raleighs from England, though my neighbour Rhona had one that was unusual, red and white. South Africa was a relatively new country, and like bicycles, many imports to South Africa originated from countries that its various immigrant communities came from, the strongest then being Britain.

On our three-speed Rudges and Raleighs, we cycled to the river, often to the Riviera Hotel, to visit a family from the United States who had come to live there, because the father was contracted to work on the building of the new oil-from-coal plant at nearby Sasolburg. It was from these new American friends, two sisters, that we learnt about toasted marshmallows. The marshmallow was put on a toasting fork and held over an open fire until it caramelized and melted slightly. Then it was placed between two slices of penny Nestlés chocolates and then two cookies and eaten. My friends and I tried this at the fireplace in our living room or 'lounge.' Because our winters were short, about two months only, most houses did not have central heating. We had the fireplace, and on winter evenings we lit a coal fire, drawing closer and closer to it as the fire waned. We had electric bar heaters in other rooms. Before supper I would take a hot-water bottle upstairs, wrap my nightclothes in it, and tuck the package under the covers, so that I would have a warm bed to go to. My sister had a hot-water bottle in the shape of a teddy bear. She played doctor with it and gave it an injection with obvious consequences!

In addition to toasting marshmallows, I learnt another thing from a visiting American, this time much later, at my university residence. We knew about Bloody Marys, but she taught us how to make a Purple Jesus with vodka and grape juice!

There was not much of a Chinese influence in South Africa, because in the apartheid years, the Chinese were classified as coloured. The Japanese, on the other hand, were classified as white, perhaps because in those times Japan had a more favourable trading relationship with South Africa. Regardless, I don't believe there any were any Japanese restaurants in my time. The few Chinese restaurants served the food banquet-style, one dish following the other, unlike the everything at once that is common practice today. Indian restaurants were quite common, but no ethnic restaurants existed in Vereeniging in my day.

Many of our clothing names came from England. They differed from the United States: for us a bag was a handbag, and a purse was something that went inside it, to hold loose change. Ladies' pants were slacks. A cardigan was usually called a jersey; a vest was a waistcoat.

Many of the flowers in our gardens also originated from England: marigolds, asters, dahlias, red salvia, larkspurs, lupines, petunias, and so on. Protea, the national flower, was not common, at least not in Vereeniging as far as I can remember. I am also not sure about Red Hot Pokers, though I think they were native to Africa. Our garden had a border of asters and petunias, and as a child I would take

White Schooldays

an aster, use the flower as a base, and thread upside-down petunia flowers onto the stem, making a crinoline of sorts for the 'ladies' with whom I played in the stories I made up.

We had a rockery in our front garden, and I played hospital with my dolls in its pools and crevices. Jacaranda trees, tropical transplants, were a signature sight in Pretoria and were quite common in nearby Johannesburg but not in my hometown. Colourful bougainvilleas, also nonindigenous, did make it to many of our front yards.

Recently my niece sent me a photograph of her daughter in Halloween costume. Halloween? What happened to Guy Fawkes Day? In my South African youth, that was the day we celebrated, another holdover from England. 'Please to remember the fifth of November, gunpowder, treason and plot.' Our activities on November 5 were not dissimilar to those for Halloween. We went around asking 'a penny for the guy,' though not in costume, and later burnt him in effigy on a neighbourhood bonfire and let off fireworks. When did one celebration morph into the next, and when did North American commercialism take over what was a fairly simple enjoyment?

Some of the original immigrant groups in South Africa were largely stereotyped by occupation: the Scots were coal miners, Greeks ran cafés, and the Portuguese, mainly from the Azores, were market gardeners. Jews—many escapees from anti-Semitism in Eastern Europe—were thought of as doctors and lawyers and financiers. I do not recall specific public festivities or celebrations that defined any of these groups.

The Malay slaves were immigrants from a more distant and exotic place, brought by the Dutch settlers as early as the mid-1600s to supply the labour needed to produce supplies for the trading vessels that stopped off en route to the East but also to produce foods for the settlers themselves.

These Malay slaves, with their Islamic feasts and fasts, their colourful language, and their foods, have had a lasting effect on the culture of the country, playing an important role in shaping the history and diversity of the region where they are congregated. The deep-rooted Coon Carnival, staged every year on the second of January, originated from their slave days when they were allowed to celebrate their only day off work in the whole year in their own manner. It has been one of their lasting and distinctive contributions.

The word 'coon' was borrowed from the United States, its pejorative and racial connotation largely ignored. As it has evolved through the decades, the Carnival has also incorporated the style and sounds of American minstrels into the celebration.

Troupes dressed in colourful shiny suits, hats, and sun umbrellas parade through downtown Cape Town singing and dancing in true Rio Carnival style.

Today the Coon Carnival is officially known as the Cape Town Minstrel Carnival, also *Kaapse Klopse*, from the Afrikaans *klop*, or beat. The participants are mostly male and are known as the Cape Coloureds, the descendants of the Malay slaves, the *slamse* or *slamaaiers*, the old Cape corruption of Malayans or Islamists, as the Muslims were referred to.

These mixed-race Cape Coloureds have always been a marginalized minority, neither black nor white, once slaves to their Dutch masters, then mistreated by the descendants of those Dutch during the apartheid regime and forced by them to relocate in racially designated areas. In postapartheid they are the second-largest South African group living in poverty, with a high illiteracy rate, a high crime rate, and strong drug-related gang activities, disillusioned by the lack of noticeable improvement in their situation in the changed post-Mandela political climate.

Yet despite their disadvantaged history, many of their rich cultural and religious traditions remain, the Coon Carnival being one of the most recognized, and every January 2, they march loudly and joyfully through the streets of Cape Town. Crowds line up on the sidewalk to watch them, seemingly unaware of what lies beneath the costumes and behind the painted faces. They enjoy the moment, giving no thought to where the singers and dancers go when Carnival is over.

Ismé Bennie

Colourfast

My early morning face has interesting colours
Eyes punched black
Lips splayed red
Unwashed last night
Waiting a deep cleanse
And another day.

APPEARANCE

Going way back in time, I can remember what I was wearing for many of the events in my life: for example, big bows in my hair for those childhood portraits in the early '40s, sitting on the piano in our house on Leslie Street. It may be that I am recalling these occasions from the actual photographs, but somehow I can feel the tightness of the knot and the silky wood of the piano.

Going back in time, I can still picture the clothes we wore through the decades of childhood and young adulthood, the '40s, '50s, and early '60s. Like other little girls, I wore hand-smocked little frocks; in winter they were made of Viyella, worn with a little vest underneath made of ribbed cotton. A larger version of the vest but with long sleeves was something called a spencer. Even adults wore these in the cold Vereeniging winter months. Toddlers graduated to pinafores and kilts and sometimes a sundress tied with bows on the shoulder, worn with matching *broekies* (panties), and in winter the occasional hand-knitted dress. My mother knitted a blue one for me and a brick-coloured one for my sister. We wore pixie caps, knitted pointed caps tied under the chin, until we were about six. They often matched a cardigan. My mother knitted all our cardigans, even those in Fair Isle. It was only when a neighbour got a knitting machine that my mother gave up knitting for us. A cardigan was something that opened down the front; a sweater was something that didn't. A pullover had no sleeves, and a waistcoat was part of a three-piece suit.

Winter in our part of South Africa was relatively cold but above freezing usually. For those short two months, we had winter coats. I remember my mother taking me to the city to buy one; it was in bluish-green tweed. I have absolutely no memory of ever wearing it or any coat at all. Heavy cardigans sufficed.

I am confused about pants or trousers; we called them slacks. Something called jeans existed in the '50s, but they were more like today's capri pants. I must have owned some pants, corduroys in winter perhaps, but pants did not play a big part in our wardrobe in those days. I know I had them at the time I went to live in the UK. A South African friend who visited me in London in 1962 asked if it was really appropriate for me to be going out wearing them!

In my teens in the '50s, big skirts became a trend, as well as dresses or skirts worn with crinolines, hoops, or heavily starched cotton petticoats. One of my summer outfits when I was about thirteen was a big floral skirt worn with a sleeveless black piqué top. Our neighbours berated my mother for letting me, a young girl, wear black.

Felt skirts, winter wear for a season or two in the '50s, were actually full circles of felt, with a hole cut in the centre for a waist. They were usually blue or red, and were often appliquéd with bright flowers or fruit.

As children, we had party dresses made of organdie and organza, eyelet, voile, faille, muslin, taffeta, georgette, and velvet, depending on the season. These were worn with little white socks, often hand-crocheted. Socks were part of our outfits until well into high school.

White Schooldays

The ballerina, strapless with a full tulle skirt, was the formal dance wear for teenage girls. The little black dress followed several years later. It was the going-out attire for young adults, for dinner or dancing.

But before that, into our later teens, straight black skirts became 'in,' worn with evening sweaters for going out. I had one of pink angora. Under the skirt we wore something called a two-way stretch, an elasticized garment that held one in tightly and sometimes had garters attached to hold up stockings. It was way before the advent of panty hose. Those were introduced in the sixties, when I was living in New York. Another undergarment of the times was the merry widow, a strapless, figure-hugging elastic foundation garment that looked like the top of a cancan costume. This was worn under strapless or low-cut dresses and could also hold up stockings. We wore very pointy bras; it seems we all wore the same style, and it was as though every girl had the same body profile, but perhaps my memory is being influenced by old movies and photographs.

We sometimes wore white gloves, perhaps just to go shopping in the city. On our feet we wore lace-ups for school and sandals the rest of the time. For games, we wore tackies (sneakers). They were always white, and to keep them pristine, they were cleaned with a white liquid, much like the Wite-Out used to correct errors pre-word processing.

Jewellery consisted mostly of charm bracelets; the more articulated the charm, the more special. We collected charms, and our arms jangled as the bracelets filled up. My set did not wear earrings. Gold hoops worn in pierced ears were considered the purview of Italian, Greek, or Portuguese kids. The children of our black maids, the women who washed and ironed our clothes, might have worn them, but we were hardly paying attention to them.

All these various styles and periods of fashion were accompanied by the hairstyle of the moment: as kids, plaits (braids) for every day and ringlets for big days. There was something called a bubble cut. At one or another time, I had an Italian boy (curls like the statue of David) or a beehive—an elaborate, teased confection that required a chopstick for scratching one's scalp inside it, or the geometric bob of the Vidal Sassoon era. Our mothers went to the hairdresser once a week in those days, sitting under the dryer, their hair set in tight pin curls or waves. I went quite often myself when I was working in Johannesburg (and later in London) to whoever the latest and most fashionable stylist was reputed to be.

We started wearing makeup when we were about fifteen, which consisted of base, face powder, rouge (blusher), lipstick, and mascara. A lipstick called Tahiti Pink stands out in my memory as *the* colour of the late '50s; it was a Day-Glow whitish pink. Helena Rubinstein cosmetics were around in the '50s. I remember breaking out in spots and thinking that using this upmarket product would clear up the problem, which was fortunately temporary. Odorono was the deodorant of the day, Prell the shampoo, and Cutex was used for nails.

Swimming costumes (aka bathing suits) were one-piece, certainly at the Vereeniging pool and on the beaches of Durban and Cape Town until perhaps the early sixties. I am not sure when the bikini became permissible wear. I know I did not have a bikini until after I returned from London in the midsixties.

I have been trying to recall what our mothers wore: housedresses as well as cotton dresses buttoned all the way down that were worn around the house; fur stoles—my mother's was fox; jeeps—boxy, wide-shouldered wool jackets that came down to midthigh. They wore two-piece suits, and I think they called them costumes.

I have some very specific memories: a pink twinset with blue Fair Isle that my mother knitted and I wore when I was about eleven to my first evening party; a dotted Swiss dress with a flared skirt that was my special Jewish New Year dress one year; it was red and had a keyhole neckline edged with white lace; a slinky, red satin dress worn on New Year's Eve to go dancing at the Navigator's Den in Cape Town; a green-and-gold dress worn to a party on Clifton Beach; it was cinched with a very wide belt (very wide belts—at least four or five inches—were a brief trend of the fifties); a black twenties-style dress that was my going-out dress at university; a turquoise taffeta dress that I wore as a bridesmaid; the black-and-white checked dress I wore on the plane on my very first trip to London.

I went off to London with a suitcase full of wide-skirted dresses; some were even sundresses. I returned to South Africa several years later with a much-pared-down wardrobe and look, defined by climate, culture, changing taste, and the passing of time.

OLD FRIENDS

My mother's chocolate cake was famous. She sent it to me at camp and to university, and a slice was usually available for a friend like Brenda on her way home from the library.

Brenda is the only friend from Vereeniging who I have in Toronto, and we get together for brunch around our birthdays, never forgetting to call each other to exchange good wishes.

When we meet, we chat about the past and whatever happened to....We look at old photographs. She is my closest local connection to those days, and we dredge up a lot of memories: about friends, about her parents who were distant, her mother's secretarial school, her brother in Israel, and so on. We stay in touch via e-mail these days and contact each other when there is news of some South African friend to share. If I hear some news—usually bad, given our ages—I tell her right away, as I did about Rachel, for instance.

I had received an e-mail from Rachel; actually it was not from her, but one she had her husband send on her behalf, because she couldn't. I phoned her as soon as I got it. We talked, and I asked what was wrong, and she replied that the doctor said it was the onset of early..., and then she could not remember early what!

I knew then. I thought of how this terrible affliction would affect her and her family, not just now but for the years ahead. I was close to tears, but crying would not have helped either of us. I was devastated that this could happen to someone with whom I was familiar, a contemporary. We are still young in today's world!

In the e-mail she dictated, she said I was still her dearest friend. She is one of my dearest friends, too, and one of my oldest. I am sad at the thought of losing my connection to her. I want to continue to share those 'Do you remembers...?' The 'Do you remembers' like when we both fancied prefects at high school, Jack and Barry, and what ever happened to them? And the tap dancing classes with Russell Meister? He was gay, but we didn't know about gay in those days. He ended up managing a hotel in the city. There was his sister Rosalie. Remember she wore a crinoline under her grey school uniform? I remember going to Rosalie's wedding at the Riviera Hotel. She had an unhappy first marriage; her husband was abusive. My old friend Dorothy told me she died recently, and her second husband was inconsolable.

I remember the blue felt skirts Rachel and I each got the year they were the fashion. Patsy Taitz had one, too, with appliqué on it. Now that's a name from the past! Patsy lived with her aunt on my street until her mother remarried, and she returned to the city, to a new family with several stepbrothers. Patsy became a nurse, not a common profession for Jewish girls at that time but often a financial choice if university was too costly. I wonder if Rachel knows what happened to Patsy. Rachel and I would ride our bicycles to the river, go together for Saturday-morning milk shakes, go shopping together in the city and to cricket matches, sitting up in the stands in the sun drinking Cokes. There is so much we have shared.

In our last year of high school, her father died, leaving her mother and four children; Rachel was the oldest. She and I served tea to the visitors who came to give condolences. We shared a lot of food experiences. We were a great cooking duo in Home Ec. We always ended up with more of whatever we made than anyone else. We baked stuff at home. There was the green-onion salad we made. I have often thought of asking if she remembers how, because I don't. But I am no longer sure what she can remember. If I have a question now, I will just have to put it away and try not to get maudlin.

Even after I left the country, Rachel and I never lost our bond. I visit her whenever I am in South Africa. We pick up our friendship as though no time has passed. At one time we talked about her financial difficulties and having to work behind the counter of a candy store with her single daughter at home, unable to find work and her children becoming ultrareligious. Life has become difficult for her as time goes on.

She once told me that she felt she had outgrown her husband. And then, some years later, things were OK again. He has recently developed problems with his eyesight. I think of the two of them having to manage together now.

I talked to my doctor once about my father who had dementia in his late years. He told me that I was the one feeling the confusion and the terror, not my father, because he couldn't.

I hope he was right!

BETWEEN THE COVERS OR MY LIFE IN BOOKS

My old friend Brenda was and still is an avid reader, as were most of my girlfriends who, like me, had learnt to read at kindergarten.

My mother took me to the library regularly to get books, nursery rhymes, fairy tales, and such. My father was proud of my reading ability and the big words I could spell when I was only about four or five.

When we moved to a house a block or two away from the library, I was able to go on my own; I was about nine then. Like most kids, Enid Blyton's *Noddy* was part of my early childhood reading. It was only much later that a naughty boy was considered a bad role model. I moved up through all the age-appropriate Enid Blytons, *The Famous Five, Malory Towers,* and so on. I read all the *Bobbsey Twins* and of course, *Just William*. There were also the *Honeybunch* books, probably long gone from library or bookstore shelves.

Ismé Bennie

My mother had always been a great reader and introduced me to all her old favourites. That's how I met my heroines: *Anne of Green Gables, Pollyanna, Heidi, Katy,* and *The Girl of the Limberlost.* I read in bed before I got up, and I remember crying over *Heidi.* Crying over a book was bad luck, according to our black maid who brought coffee up every morning early, as did maids in most white South African homes in those days. Books I loved and remember clearly to this day are *Daddy Long Legs*; of course, *Little Women* and its sequels; and especially Noel Streatfield's *Ballet Shoes* and *White Boots.* Skating was not an activity with which we identified, given South Africa's climate. But like many girls, I did aspire to be a ballerina, and I did go to ballet classes as a child. I was never any good, daydreaming at the *barre*.

I am not sure when I read *Black Beauty*. It was banned in South Africa because of the words 'black' and 'beauty' in the title. There are no black people in the book, since it is set in nineteenth-century England. It is actually about a horse. But in the apartheid era, it was censored because its title suggested it was some kind of antigovernment propaganda.

National Velvet was a horse book that was acceptable, and so was the film. I followed Elizabeth Taylor's life in the movie magazines of the day. I also cut out pictures of Gregory Peck from them and pinned them on my bedroom wall. Who knew? But before movie magazines, there were Enid Blyton's weekly *Sunny Stories* and also *Girl's Own*, with its mix of articles and stories designed to educate and improve. My mother subscribed to *Woman's Own*, a British lifestyle magazine, and we knitted from its patterns.

In our early teens, my friends and I shared a love for *Nancy Drew, Cherry Ames,* and *The Hardy Boys*. The best birthday present was a new *Hardy Boys* mystery. As I write, I wonder if any of the books I mention strike chords today. In a Toronto cookbook store a few weeks ago, I saw *The Nancy Drew Cookbook*, and so I know that at least one name is still around.

White Schooldays

We didn't have television in South Africa until many years later, and radio was all we knew for a long time. So I related to the book *Lark Radio Singer*. It was one of a series of books about careers for women, like journalism and moviemaking, careers that would have seemed exotic to local girls like me, South Africa being so far away from the mainstream world. I am writing about the '40s and '50s. Girls like me became teachers or librarians or possibly physiotherapists; others took up nursing, more I think for financial reasons than out of a sense of vocation.

In my high-school years, I started reading Mills and Boon romances in their distinctive brown covers, and I anxiously awaited the latest. When I was about twelve or thirteen, I secretly visited a bookstore and bought a sex education book, called something like *Growing Up for Girls*. I took it with me when my father and I visited my friend Dorothy's parents up the street. Dorothy and I would closet ourselves in her bedroom and pore over it, trying to find out what sex was all about. We tried to get our hands on 'daring' books. *Forever Amber* would have been one. We skimmed through them looking for the sexy bits. South Africa was very conservative; 'indecent,' 'obscene,' and 'objectionable' were standards often applied to books and movies.

I did move on to more adult novels, sharing these with my mother and my friends, books like Pearl Buck's *The Good Earth*; Han Suyin's *A Many-Splendoured Thing*, Howard Spring's *Fame is the Spur*, and Marcia Davenport's *My Brother's Keeper*. And of course, Daphne DuMaurier's *Rebecca* and *My Cousin Rachel*. Many of these were tearjerkers, and most were filmed. I cried as I read and cried even more in the cinema.

These and the early books of my youth fired my imagination, and they still evoke the same emotions in me. I was young when I read them, but they affected my perception of the world and my outlook on life.

AN AFRICAN BIBLIOGRAPHY

I look out for stories about Africa, both actual and fictional. I love those set in the romantic colonial period, with protagonists like Beryl Markham and Isak Dinesen. And every now and then, a modern soul mate appears, like Alexandra Fuller, whose coming-of-age story, *Don't Let's Go to the Dogs Tonight,* describes life with her unconventional family in Rhodesia, now Zimbabwe, during the uncertainties in that part of the world in the late '70s.

But it is those novels set specifically in South Africa that resonate with me, as they touch on my own life growing up in a small town. There was a tremendous feeling of recognition when I first read Nadine Gordimer's *The Lying Days*. Set in the earlier years of apartheid, it tells the story of a young woman's emotional and intellectual journey into womanhood and paints a vivid picture of the narrow-mindedness of small-town life and the racism that pervades it. Like me, the heroine is the daughter of a conventional middle-class family living in an all-white community near a mine (gold in her case; ours was coal). Her political consciousness is awakened once she meets people outside her normal circle and by her love affair with a liberal-thinking young man. I don't believe the book triggered any great political awakening in me. I was about seventeen, the same age as Nadine Gordimer's heroine at the start of the book when I first read it. I thought of myself as liberal, but my own political awareness came after living abroad. Like Doris Lessing's Martha Quest in *The Four-Gated City*, I left Africa for London and experienced a new world.

Lynn Freed's heroine in *Home Ground* also chose to leave the country, wanting to escape her growing discomfort with the country's racism and to free herself from her family—prosperous, flamboyant, and noisy theatre people, very different from my ordinary family. She has had to come to terms with two realities: being Jewish in a predominantly gentile society and being white in an overwhelmingly black country. For me, these were not issues I faced in my growing-up years. It was several decades later when the novel appeared that I found some common ground.

In reading these biographies and memoirs and coming-of-age novels, I keep looking for similarities; how does my South African coming-of-age compare? As I child I had no real political consciousness, cocooned in comfortable, white small-town life, but now the adult me is encountering pictures of apartheid seen through a child's eyes: a boy in Mark Behr's *The Smell of Apples* who has to deal with the deeply ingrained racial attitudes indoctrinated into his generation; Michiel Heyns's character Simon in *The Children's Day*, set in a small town in the 1960s, in which the son of an English father and an Afrikaans mother has to deal with the problems his mixed parentage creates in a country where hostility exists between the so-called English upper class and the lesser Afrikaners. These books are by white South Africans about white South Africans. In recent times, their black counterparts are being written, but I am looking to compare, not contrast.

I go back to South Africa through the years, like Alexander Fuller in her sequel and Lynn Freed's character in hers. We go back to visit the family we left behind but also to test our childhood memories. Some things like colours, smells, tastes, and sounds don't change but a society can and has, and I go back to a different country.

THE NEW SOUTH AFRICA

I get a picture of today's South Africa from the emerging South African crime writers, whose novels provide a view of the country through new and different eyes. In the '70s, in the height of the apartheid era, James McClure wrote groundbreaking police procedurals featuring the partnership of a black and a white detective and containing a strong message about the inequalities of a society divided along racial lines. But it took until the mid-1990s for a new crop of writers to appear on the literary scene, writing with gritty realism and painting evocative pictures of the country today. I look forward to new books by Deon Meyer, Roger Smith, Michael Stanley, and others. I travel with their protagonists to the city of Cape Town with its winding roads under the shadow of Table Mountain, to the port city of Durban and to the semidesert Karoo, places I have known. Inherent in their books are reminders of the injustices of the apartheid era, and their books highlight with stark reality the everyday issues that exist in the new South Africa: poverty, crime, violence, and corruption in high places.

While most white South Africans just try to get on with their lives in an environment largely isolated from these harsh realities, my sister Pauline, who still lives in South Africa, has been directly touched by them.

I visit her in South Africa, in the city where I worked and studied. It feels the same to me, even in these postapartheid years. I stay with her in her apartment in a gated community in the affluent white suburbs, reminiscent of Beverley Hills, and drive with her to upmarket shopping malls and restaurants.

Like most white South Africans, she still has black help, but weekly not daily. My sister's help is Alida. My sister has my mother's caring nature. She organizes the fixings for Alida's children's birthdays, buys the oldest girl jeans and some of the trendier clothes a teenager wants. She helps her with her homework. On hot days she takes cold drinks to the men who man the security gate of her apartment complex. She tips liberally. She bought baby necessities when Alida was pregnant last year. During her maternity leave, Lorna filled in. In December 2009 to be exact, my sister's apartment was broken into; she was stabbed, strangled, and robbed. She has healed physically and has done remarkably well emotionally, but the scar will be there forever, particularly as there is no closure once the culprits disappear into a huge black hole that is Johannesburg. Does my sister think it was a random attack? Two days before, Lorna had asked her for 2000 Rand (about CAD$300). My sister refused. While—relatively speaking—my sister is far better off, she has little discretionary cash, and this was an excessive request. She believes the attack was one of revenge.

On the plus side, the incident has brought my sister closer to her children, who have been saddened by the experience and their brush with mortality. We've all been personally touched. For me, the afternoon thunderstorms, the smell of the red earth, the magnificent sunsets, the creaking of houses settling down for the night, these things—so much part of my South African consciousness—have been overtaken by a new and ever-present wakefulness.

Epilogue

Waiting for Mandela

When Mandela died, in the emotion and turmoil of the media coverage, I thought a lot about life in South Africa: life in the apartheid years of my growing up and then, life in South Africa experienced as a visitor and observer from afar, from Canada, in these five decades since I left the country of my birth.

In the wake of his death, Mandela's achievements have been justly praised. He managed to maintain a state of peace and forgiveness in a racially divided society, keeping a bloody revolution at bay, but I still long for what was almost impossible to bring about, what could have been possible had decades of apartheid not intervened—a country of promise for all!

Though his life as a fighter of apartheid began in the '50s, Mandela was not a name that conjured up any political awareness in the years of my coming-of-age, the '40s and '50s in the small-town South Africa I try to put down on paper. My generation was politically innocent and unaware, and separation of the races, good or bad, was not a factor in our lives. Yet as we went about our daily business as privileged whites under the southern sun, I sometimes wonder whether for many of us in our subconscious there was a recognition, a longing, a need for a different South Africa. In essence we were 'waiting for Mandela.'

I happened to be in South Africa a week or so after his release from imprisonment on Robben Island. The country was euphoric, excited, and light-hearted. His release epitomized the possibility that equality for all could be attained. A little of that hope has lingered, though diminishing as the years go by. I still look upon Mandela as a guardian angel of sorts, despite the fact that my family was a direct victim of crime and violence during his tenure, a tenure during which crime and violence and corruption escalated. I am not sanguine, but I hope the spirit of his guardianship remains over South Africa's political and social life in the years ahead.

Will South Africa seem any different now, when I go back to visit? Life for whites in the affluent, white, northern suburbs of Johannesburg is superficially the same—shopping malls full of international brand names, high-end cars on the streets, fine residences with landscaped gardens, and household help who are still black. Of course, service in stores and banks and offices is now multiracial, houses have heavy security with bars and gates, and people pay to have their cars watched while they go about their errands. The infrastructure has suffered from power outages and downed phone lines, but people cope. For many whites—and a small number of blacks—it is still a very good life.

Mandela has gone, but as always, I am in constant touch with South Africa, with friends, and with my sister and her family who have remained there. Our phone calls and e-mails deal with our everyday lives, the movies we have seen, the books we are reading, holiday plans, news about relatives, work, and the weather. There is no political content to our communication. But lingering in the background is a collective feeling of loss, a vision of a South Africa without Mandela!

Acknowledgments

Some of the pieces in this collection were originally published in the *Maple Tree Literary Supplement*, albeit in different forms, and my thanks go to mtls.ca Managing Editor Amatoritsero Ede for giving me the opportunity to be read and to the readers whose comments encouraged and inspired me to keep writing.

My thanks also go to Michael Levine, lawyer, agent, and friend, for his continued interest and support.

Thanks also to friends and relatives who have kept me in touch with my roots. In the interest of privacy, a few first names have been changed.

The creative writing courses I took at The University of Toronto. Humber College, and The Art Gallery of Ontario gave me the confidence to write in my own voice.

About the Author

A graduate of the University of the Witwatersrand in South Africa, Ismé began her professional life as a librarian. Moving to North America and to television, she became one of the most respected women in Canadian broadcasting, widely recognized for her contributions to the television industry. In 1990, she received the Canadian Film and Television Production Association (CFTPA) Personal Achievement Award and in 1995, the CFTPA Jack Chisholm Award for Lifetime Contribution to the Motion Picture and Television Industry. In 2003, Women in Film and Television—Toronto (WIFT—T) honoured her with the Outstanding Achievement Award for her role as a trailblazer for women in the television industry.

After giving up full-time employment, she has focused on writing. In addition to memoir pieces about growing up in South Africa, she has also published factual articles on a variety of subjects from food to crime fiction. She also contributes regularly to New York-based *VideoAge International* on aspects of the Canadian media scene.

Notes

The following references were either quoted directly in the text or provide additional background:

Foreword
- *Maple Tree Literary Supplement* 2008 - present. www.mtls.ca

Other Friends
- 'smile of content' – source unknown

'You Must Remember This...'
- title from *As Time Goes By*. Words and music by Herman Hupfeld

My Dinner With Mordecai
- Foran, Charles. *Mordecai: The Life and Times*. Knopf Doubleday Canada, 2010

George or Holidays by the Sea

'in stomme bewondering' from *Repos Ailleurs* by Totius (Jacob Daniel du Toit) 1877-1953.

High School
- 'Maar daardie merk wort grooter' from *Vergewe en Vergeet* by Totius

Taste Buds
- 'the quality of mercy' - from *The Merchant of Venice* by William Shakespeare
- Mary Higham. Household Cookery For South Africa. Central News Agency, Ltd. Eleventh edition 1947

Reading; An African Bibliography; The New South Africa

For additional information on books mentioned in the above, see my articles in www.suite101.net
- *Classic Novels for Girls*
- *More Classic Novels for girls*
- *A South African Childhood: Five writer's Stories*

Ismé Bennie

- *Coming of Age in Apartheid South Africa*
- *African Memoirs: Love Stories about a Continent*
- *Crime Fiction from Southern Africa: An Introduction*

Made in the USA
Monee, IL
26 April 2021